OTHER TITLES OF INTEREST FROM ST. LUCIE PRESS

Mastering the Diversity Challenge: Easy On-the-Job Applications for Measurable Results

The Cost of Bad Hiring Decisions and How to Avoid Them

Reengineering the Training Function: How to Align Training with the New Corporate Agenda

Creating Productive Organizations

Leadership by Encouragement

The New Leader: Bringing Creativity to the Workplace

The Motivating Team Leader

Organization Teams: Building Continuous Quality Improvement

Team Building: A Structured Learning Approach

For more information about these titles call, fax or write:

St. Lucie Press
100 E. Linton Blvd., Suite 403B
Delray Beach, FL 33483

TEL (561) 274-9906 • FAX (561) 274-9927
E-MAIL information@slpress.com
WEB SITE http://www.slpress.com

S^t_L

D1551548

Your
Outplacement
Handbook
Redesigning Your Career

Your
Outplacement
Handbook
Redesigning Your Career

Fern Lebo

S^t_L

St. Lucie Press
Delray Beach, Florida

Printed and bound in the U.S.A. Printed on acid-free paper.
10 9 8 7 6 5 4 3 2 1

ISBN 1-57444-029-2

Direct all inquiries to St. Lucie Press, Inc., 100 E. Linton Blvd., Suite 403B, Delray Beach, Florida 33483.

Phone: (561) 274-9906
Fax: (561) 274-9927
E-mail: information@slpress.com
Web site: http://www.slpress.com

S^{t}L

Published by
St. Lucie Press
100 E. Linton Blvd., Suite 403B
Delray Beach, FL 33483

TABLE OF CONTENTS

PREFACE

It used to be an employee prepared for a job, went to work, followed the rules, and looked forward to a long and stable future within the organization. It used to be that when you were hired, you knew exactly what the work entailed and precisely what skills and abilities were required to move you up the organizational ladder. It used to be an employee demonstrated loyalty and a "nose to the grindstone" attitude and could count on a future in which the organization would repay that loyalty with support, career guidance, and the promise of security. That's what used to be.

In today's world of organizational renewal, what used to be just isn't anymore. Company loyalty to the faithful employee seems to have gone the way of T-Rex. Job security is a curious phrase left over from the dinosaur era. Indeed, career planning is often left in the very hands holding the pink slip.

Still, many organizations do feel a sense of responsibility to their loyal employees who must, because of organizational change or marketplace realities, replan their future or design their own career.

For the Organization

Your Outplacement Handbook provides answers and direction for employees working within an organization or for those on their way out.

As a concerned member of a human resources department or as a conscientious manager or leader, you will want to put *Your Outplacement Handbook* on every desk for every person because it is no longer possible or reasonable for your organization to assist with career pathing and personal development issues. You may use this manual as a support text in outplacement seminars, offer it to people before their exit interview, or distribute it to your staff as a personal growth tool.

A responsible organization provides career planning resources for its employees and assists employees so they are in a position to take responsibility for themselves. Whether you are rightsizing or outplacing, reorganizing or flattening—or not—every employee in your organization deserves the opportunity to explore their individual potential for skill transfer and career redesign. Offer *Your Outplacement Handbook* as a standard self-development manual because your organization cares about its people.

For the Manual User

What with restructuring, reorganization, re-engineering, downsizing, rightsizing, and retrenchment, the prospect of finding a great job, a job precisely like the one you've been dreaming of, is slim. The Department of Labor recently reported that people can expect five career changes in a lifetime. And indeed, for the first time in their lives, many qualified, talented, and deserving workers are suddenly finding themselves buffeted by the turbulence of job loss.

Still, whether you are currently employed or not, you need to be career wise. When it comes to flying high, we believe that attitude, not aptitude, determines your altitude. Shoot for the stars. If you land on the moon, that's not bad!

Your Outplacement Handbook confronts the issues and helps you to find honest, applicable, and pragmatic solutions. It provides an opportunity for personal growth, for maintaining self-esteem, and for developing a hands-on, effective plan of attack for moving forward in today's mercurial marketplace. If you are one of the fortunate who is still gainfully employed and you are interested in developing your own career path, this book will equip you with an in-depth plan of attack.

Pasteur said that chance favors the prepared mind. In working through this book, you are preparing yourself for the challenges and opportunities ahead. So, if luck is when preparation meets opportunity, then you are certainly in luck!

Working through the book, you will discover a variety of opportunities, challenges, and surprises. You may come to a new understanding of who you are, who you want to be, and where you want to go. You will begin to realize that every decision is a career decision.

The trick to being happily employed is to "single track" your personal vision with your working reality—to synthesize hopes, aspirations, and actuality. The late author and teacher Joseph Campbell put it well: "follow your bliss."

Happily, as you move through the process, you will develop a practical plan and a valuable skill set that move you towards your elusive future. So be positive, be optimistic, be reassured. As Judy Issokson, Instructional Conscience at Sun Microsystems, says, "It's possible that whatever you do next hasn't even been invented yet."

The good news:

1. There are more work options and opportunities than ever.

2. While there are fewer secure jobs, there is lots of work to be done.

3. Lateral moves within your organization may be an excellent way to advance your career.

4. Small businesses provide more job opportunities than ever before.

5. There are more successful home businesses today than at any time in history.

Acknowledgments

I would like to express my heartfelt appreciation to Marilynn Burke, M.Ed., who freely provided thoughtful guidance, sound input, and honest feedback in the preparation of this book. My affection and special thanks to Bram Lebo, LLB, MBA, MBI, for his assistance in the preparation of this book and for his contribution of the chapter on Job Hunting for Recent Graduates. For his expertise, patience, and assistance with graphics, I renew my thanks to Jay Lebo, my Information Systems Specialist, and, once again, offer a sincere "thank you" to Lewis Eisen, LLB, for his help with editing.

I also wish to recognize the invaluable contributions of the knowledgable authors who generously allowed me to excerpt from their published materials and to the enthusiastic job searchers who provided me with samples of their on-line resumes.

About the Author

Fern Lebo is president of Lebo Communications (http://www.interlog.com/~flebo/home.htm), an innovative company providing consultation and training in support of career pathing, management development and personal growth initiatives. She partners with a broad variety of public and private sector clients across North America and creates customized, results-driven programs to support new directions. Her professional training as a psychotherapist brings an expert's insights and approach to the materials she develops. Her focus is on enabling individuals to achieve self-actualization through the design and pursuit of a career that "fits."

An internationally published author, Fern has written innumerable articles and several books, among them, *Mastering the Diversity Challenge: Easy On-the-Job Applications for Measurable Results.*

SECTION I

TAKING CHARGE

SURVIVAL TACTICS

Happiness is self-contentedness.
—Aristotle, C. 300 BCE
Career Carpentry

Employees who have jobs which are truly satisfying are assets to the organizations that employ them. If you are presently working, managing your career may mean shaping your current position, influencing your manager, using your skills in a new and different way, or developing new skills. You may need to discover the position in your company for which you are better suited, or you may need to leave your current organization and look outside.

If, like many other employed people, you have left the planning of your career to others, you may be committing a serious error in judgment. No matter how supportive, encouraging, or caring your organization appears to be, the truth is that no one cares as much about you as you do. No matter how paternalistic your organization is, or was, in looking after the needs of its employees, an organization simply cannot do the superior job that you can do in planning your future.

You are reading this book because you know the importance of taking charge and managing the career planning process for yourself. No one else can do it better; no one else knows the real you as well as you do.

Wherever you may be on your life's journey, it is typically distressing and painful to find yourself suddenly adrift in an unfamiliar sea. This book is about taking charge, about controlling the currents and getting

3

both feet back on solid ground. It is about taking command of the steering so that you:

☺ end up where you want to be

☺ shape your own destiny

☺ manage your fate

☺ cease reacting to external realities, life events, and other people's opinions about what you should be and begin a proactive process

☺ overcome the real and perceived barriers to your success.

Most people do not intuitively know where to begin such a process. *Your Outplacement Handbook* helps you to plot your course. It provides everything you need to design your own future and to take the specific action steps that move you forward. Skills are immediately applicable, and the guide is rich in practical pay-offs.

Objective

Working your way through this manual will help you to:

1. "single track" your vision and your reality; build your own career

2. increase your sense of being in charge of your future

3. ask yourself important questions that help you get in touch with real answers

4. access your allies

5. determine the interests, skills, personality, and values that you have to offer a future employer

6. identify the kind of work and type of environment in which you would be most satisfied and successful

7. prepare for a successful job search by deciding what should be highlighted in your resume

8. discover how best to answer questions in an employment interview

9. write sensational letters and the "ideal" resume

10. create an effective Career Action Plan.

You will want to attack this process the way you would like to attack life—with enthusiasm, energy, and an inquiring mind. Set aside a specific time to work your way through this book—perhaps three or four hours a week—and stick to your timetable. Work in a specific "work area" you have defined and keep all your paperwork in a notebook or folder. Attack the exercises as you would a new job, with an earnest interest in learning and developing a new skill set. If some of the exercises at first glance seem unimportant, do them anyway. You are the only one who will ever see them, and you never know what hidden gem you may discover in your search.

Many people believe that success is not a destination, but is a manner of traveling. Should you choose to start this journey, the process will be a rewarding experience in itself, and, equally important, it will produce results.

2

GETTING STARTED:
THE CAREER AND LIFE PLANNING PROCESS

Personal mastery is the discipline of continually clarifying and deepening our personal vision, of focusing our energies, of developing patience, and of seeing reality objectively.

—Peter M. Senge

To exist is to change, to change is to mature, to mature is to go on creating oneself endlessly.

—Henri Bergson

This manual addresses the career or life planning process and is comprised of two major sections. Section I, *Taking Charge*, focuses on self-knowledge and career knowledge. **Self-knowledge** is the first essential component to redesigning your career and includes understanding:

☺ your personal style (what are my personality traits?)

☺ your values (what is important to me?)

☺ your interests (what do I enjoy?)

☺ your abilities, aptitudes, and skills (what can I do or learn to do?)

Self-knowledge comes together like pieces of a puzzle. You begin with interesting fragments of the picture and perhaps some idea of the expected outcome. But it is the fitting together of those bits and pieces that gives you the complete picture.

Career knowledge is the second component you need for redesigning your career. Once you have an in-depth understanding of yourself, your style, and your needs and wants, you must then be aware of the employment options available, the changing economy and work environment, and the skills, education, and approach necessary for success. Career knowledge includes understanding:

- the new economy

- alternative workstyles

- education

- occupations

- leisure.

Section II, *Taking Action*, focuses on making it happen—turning your vision into reality—the third essential component for redesigning your career. It includes traditional and nontraditional job search techniques, outlines, and samples of every kind of letter you will need including cover letters, follow-up letters, and thank you notes, and detailed formats and samples of traditional and electronic or Key Word resumes. It gives you telephone tips, interview procedures, and networking strategies. In addition, there is a step-by-step Career Action Plan for you to use.

Should you decide, after completing Section I, that you would really prefer to be self-employed, Section II offers detailed guidance for the entrepreneur and hints for starting your own business.

Everything you need to know about where to look, how to look, and what steps to follow is provided—with lots of tips, pointers, and suggestions from the "experts" in career transition. I have also provided the Internet World Wide Web address or the Internet e-mail address for each of these authorities, so you have all the guidance you could possibly need here.

3

LOOKING BACK TO THE FUTURE

That's what learning is. You suddenly understand something you've understood all your life, but in a new way.

—Doris Lessing

Focusing In

As in any process, you must start somewhere, and your first task is to focus. Let's start with an exploration of your past, because in looking back, you will begin to identify the key qualities of things you value and want to consider for the future.

Sifting through past experiences helps to reveal your unique and diverse likes, dislikes, strengths, and weaknesses. In other words, you will begin to create a personal profile that defines a list of things you want and need in your work—your criteria for being happily employed.

You may presume you already know this information, but research tells us that thinking through the answers to each question and writing them down helps you to clarify and focus—plus it promises new and important insights. At the very least, working through the exercises may reaffirm your suspicions.

EXERCISE 1

Exploring Aptitudes: Revealing the Real Me

Answer these questions for each of the following periods in your life (if you are still a young adult, omit the last).

- child

- adolescent

- young adult

- older adult

AS A CHILD

1. What are some of the things I liked to do (hobbies and interests)?

2. Why did I like them?

3. What qualities or satisfactions did they have for me?

4. What skills did I bring to the task?

5. What was my favorite subject in school/work?

6. Why did I like it?

7. Why was I good at it?

8. What jobs have I had (chores, work experiences—paid or unpaid)? What were my duties? What did I like? What did I not like?

AS AN ADOLESCENT

1. What are some of the things I liked to do (hobbies and interests)?

2. Why did I like them?

3. What qualities or satisfactions did they have for me?

4. What skills did I bring to the task?

5. What was my favorite subject in school/work?

6. Why did I like it?

7. Why was I good at it?

8. What jobs have I had (chores, work experiences, paid or unpaid)? What were my duties? What did I like? What did I not like?

AS A YOUNG ADULT

1. What are some of the things I like to do (hobbies and interests)?

2. Why do I like them?

3. What qualities or satisfactions do they have for me?

4. What skills do I bring to the task?

5. What is my favorite topic/activity in school/work?

6. Why do I like it?

7. Why am I good at it?

8. What jobs do I have (chores, work experiences, paid or unpaid)? What are my duties? What do I like? What do I not like?

AS AN OLDER ADULT

1. What are some of the things I like to do (hobbies and interests)?

2. Why do I like them?

3. What qualities or satisfactions do they have for me?

4. What skills do I bring to the task?

5. What is my favorite topic/activity in school/work?

6. Why do I like it?

7. Why am I good at it?

8. What jobs do I have (chores, work experiences, paid or unpaid)? What are my duties? What do I like? What do I not like?

CHILD

	JOB	DUTIES	LIKED	DISLIKED
1				
2				
3				
4				
5				
6				
7				

ADOLESCENT

	JOB	DUTIES	LIKED	DISLIKED
1				
2				
3				
4				
5				
6				
7				

YOUNG ADULT

	JOB	DUTIES	LIKED	DISLIKED
1				
2				
3				
4				
5				
6				
7				

OLDER ADULT

	JOB	DUTIES	LIKED	DISLIKED
1				
2				
3				
4				
5				
6				
7				

Summary

1. What jobs/careers did I once think of doing?

   _____

   _____

2. Why did I consider those jobs/careers attractive? What was
   the "turn on"?

   _____

   _____

3. What are some jobs or careers I think I might like to do in
   the future? Why does each appeal to me?

   _____

   _____

	JOB or CAREER	WHY
1		
2		
3		
4		

CONNECTING TO THE NEW ECONOMY

Only Connect.
—E.M. Forester

Focusing Out

Statistics say that you are going to work 90,000 hours before you retire. Scary, perhaps, but true. Shouldn't you know what's going on out there?

> **Key Features of the New Economy**
>
> **Global Communication**
>
> **Technology**
>
> **Quality-of-Life Focus**
>
> **Personal Growth Issues**
>
> **Changing Workplace**
>
> **Demographics**

Global Communication

Before the age of mass communication, people were neither informed nor aware of very much outside of their own little villages. It often took weeks, months, or even years for news from a far-off land to crawl across the globe. But with the advent of mass communications, the world as we know it has become a global village. News travels instantly. Jobs are advertised internationally. People jet from one side of the earth to the other in a matter of hours. Commodities move across continents and over the sea at a dizzying speed. Still, you may not be fully aware of the profound impact of global communication on you.

To the evolution in technology, mass communication, and travel add the crumbling of trade barriers and newly opened borders. From that mix arises a new age of global competition. That means that at any given time, in any given place, there are new markets opening. In addition, there is a frantic desire on the part of business to improve productivity, to increase flexibility, and to lower costs to a competitive level. Sophisticated, instantaneous telecommunications networks throughout the world mean that anyone, including you, can do business anywhere at any time (right from your basement, if you like). It also means that work itself, and the way we do the work, are changing, too.

Technology

If you can think of a job, virtually any job, you can bet that it has been seriously affected by the technological revolution. The results, in the big picture, are that fewer jobs are being better handled by fewer workers than ever before. Productivity has increased because those fewer workers are working harder to compensate for cuts to middle layers.

Though work is tougher, the quality of work has risen. At one time, we paid highly intelligent people to sit and mechanically calculate numbers for us. Today, machines can do that; the people spend their time thinking about what the numbers mean and how to act on them.

We don't use people anymore to transport information; it's too expensive. It is much cheaper to transport the information electronically and use the people to interpret the information itself.

Quality-of-Life Focus

No matter where you look, you are bombarded by information with a seemingly new focus—quality of life. Politicians exhort their constituents to remember family values; smoking has become a social taboo, and health and fitness clubs are sprouting like dandelions. Efforts to save the whale, rescue the reef, and protect the panda make headlines. Aids to health and nutrition have crept into the New York Stock Exchange. While all of this is happening, we are invited to become friends of the wilderness and caretakers of our planet. The quality-of-life concept has expanded to include health, fitness, family, the environment, and much more. This new thrust has opened business opportunities never before imagined.

With the increased awareness in environmental issues, there is a major move to clean up. There is a whole untapped source of work waiting to be done in supporting a cleaner and safer environment and in developing the technology to make that happen. But that's not all there is to quality of life.

Entire industries have been spawned around concern for the depletion of the ozone layer. There is sunscreen in beauty products and insect repellents; the millenary industry is enjoying a stunning revival as hats come back in fashion; new sunscreening fabrics have been created for clothing, tents, and protective or decorative canopies. There are fitness facilities, personal trainers, resorts, spas, and adventure holidays. There is concern about the air we breathe, the water we drink, the wood we use, and the plastics, diapers and garbage we discard. Indeed, there are businesses whose very existence could not have been conceived only decades ago.

Our social expectations have changed. Working at home is now a reasonable and rational alternative. It is acceptable to have part-time employment—especially for caregivers, and the threshold of physical comfort has improved.

Personal Growth Issues

No longer do we consider an individual's education completed with the receipt of a diploma or a degree. Both on-the-job and outside the workplace, people have begun to think of learning as a lifelong pursuit.

Look around and you will find there is a recognition that intellectual stimulation, skill building, and personal development are enriching endeavors, perhaps life-altering experiences. There is a return to learning, both formally and informally, as a route to spending leisure time in a way that helps an individual to self-actualize or as a means to improving life or career prospects. Computer lessons have become as routine as driving lessons. Psychotherapy sessions are as common as tennis instruction or sewing classes.

It is universally acknowledged that the only constant in today's world is change. Constant change means constant learning. But constant learning does not necessarily mean constant schooling. It means taking responsibility for your own education by keeping informed, adding to and upgrading your skills set, and being aware of new opportunities and changing demands.

Demographics

Our population is aging, and its face is changing dramatically. Presently, approximately 10% of the population is over 65. In 40 years, about 25% of the population will be over 65. The current need for two-income families, the relative ease of travel, the advent of multi-national companies that move their employees around the globe, and the reality of increased immigration all mean that the workforce composition is changing.

Changing Workplace

You know as much as anyone about the massive reorganization and downsizing efforts recently undertaken by many major organizations. You, in fact, may be one of the many suffering the consequences of the changing workplace. And, as a result of outplacement, de-hiring, or any other euphemism you may choose, more people than ever are out there.

In their search for paid employment, people may be consulting to businesses, they may be looking for contract work, or they may be telecommuting to an office that has physically been downsized or no longer exists. Where they work, how they work, and at what they work may also change from project to project. Frank Ogden, the well-known futurist, describes this paradigm shift in how and where work is being done as "a bulldozer of change."

You must be aware of how and in what direction the workplace is changing in order to design a successful career plan for yourself. You need to understand the look of "The New Organization" if you wish to find your place in it.

No more than two or three years ago, 54% of all work was to be found in traditional jobs. Today, 50% of work is in traditional jobs, and 50% is in alternative forms of employment such as term positions, seasonal work that changes with the weather, self-employment, shared jobs, part-time work, and short-term contracted positions. Alternative employment also includes telecommuting, skill and talent sharing to create virtual companies, consulting, and entrepreneurial work.

Put another way, 50% of the workforce does not go to the same place every morning for a specified number of regular hours to perform more or less the same work on a daily basis for an indefinite period of time.

Clearly, there is a shift from full-time traditional work to alternative types of employment, and the next five years will continue to impact the percentages even more dramatically. Still, no matter what you want to do, almost all employment opportunities rely on transferable skills such as literacy, math skills, communication skills, basic computer skills, people-handling skills, and a positive attitude.

Preparing for Today's Economy

While you work at the serious business of career or life planning, you must have an understanding of today's economy to help you make informed decisions. In her book *Shifting Gears*, Nuala Beck reports on "The Engines of the New Economy." She says that the future of work lies, to a great degree, in the following fields:

COMPUTERS and SEMICONDUCTORS

- semiconductors
- computer equipment and software
- information services

HEALTH and MEDICAL

- medical care and diagnostics

- pharmaceuticals

- surgical/medical instruments

- biotechnology

COMMUNICATIONS and TELECOMMUNICATIONS

- telecommunications services

- guided missiles and space equipment

- radio and microwave communications

- entertainment industry

INSTRUMENTATION

- optical instruments and lenses

- engineering and scientific equipment

- process controls

- environmental consulting and equipment

The preceding list may be up-to-date today but is likely to be outdated as soon as tomorrow—such is our changing reality. But as William Bridges explains in his book *Job Shift*, if we stop to review the history of jobs, we discover that the concept of having a job has evolved over centuries.

In the Agricultural Era, critics claimed that "the job" was a socially dangerous idea. They believed that would draw working hands away from the fields where they were most needed and that the daily routine of going to a job would decimate the wholesome family structure as we knew it.

Later, with the advent of the Industrial Age, we were urged to find jobs as a method of raising our country's standard of living and as a means to becoming valuable and contributing wage earners.

Now, in the Information Era, we are hooked on jobs; across the country, there is an outcry about the lack of jobs and pressure on government and individuals to create jobs, because there is a belief that everyone deserves a job!

But, the world is changing again, and **while there are fewer and fewer jobs, there is lots of work to do**. In this new world order, you need a vision of what is possible.

THE EVOLUTION OF THE JOB

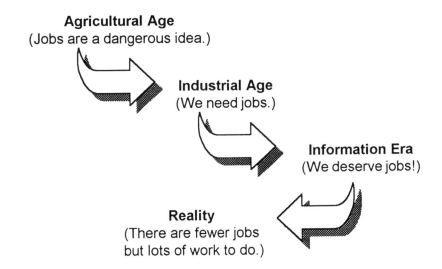

Agricultural Age
(Jobs are a dangerous idea.)

Industrial Age
(We need jobs.)

Information Era
(We deserve jobs!)

Reality
(There are fewer jobs but lots of work to do.)

MAKING CONNECTIONS

All things are connected!
The beauty of living is looking for connections.

The well-known author of *Managing Transitions*, William Bridges, reminds us that change and the rate of change are more dynamic today than ever. A personal assessment is a dynamic activity, too. It takes looking back, looking forward, and looking sideways. It means examining everything subjectively and objectively, with a microscope and with a telescope—until all the connections become dazzlingly clear.

Discovering Motivating Patterns

The answers you gave in Exercise 1 are just a beginning. Set the exercise aside for now; you will need to rethink it now and later to search for common themes or threads.

For example, in working through this process, you might discover that you enjoyed activities where you could focus on a task in solitude, without interruption. Closer examination might reveal that you liked all the tasks that involved working with your hands, using your manual dexterity, or paying attention to detail. Perhaps as a child, you were thrilled to win a soapbox design contest.

When you look back and explore the reasons for your excitement, you realize that while you liked the recognition of winning, most of all you enjoyed working alone to achieve your success. As a result, you were motivated to enter a number of design contests. Compare these discoveries to your other entries and look for themes. In the soapbox example, the themes are recognition, independence, creativity, and manual dexterity.

Summarize the themes you have found. These **THINGS I VALUE** are your drivers or *motivating patterns*, your turn-ons, and the sources of your life satisfaction. They might include things like money, personal freedom, solid friendships, or a fancy car. Whatever you choose, they are your choices.

EXERCISE 2

Things I Value

_____

_____

_____

_____

_____

_____

_____

_____

_____

_____

_____

_____

_____

Clarifying Values

We tend to lock into our memories things that have had negative or uncomfortable feelings about them. Ask anyone what they dislike about their job, their friends, or their last vacation, and they can usually produce an immediate list of negatives. But because it is easy to get trapped in negatives, we will explore the positives, too—that's part of the process.

The next page is a continuation of Exercise 1. It asks you to examine your last job and detail the specifics you disliked about it. Start by using the power of your memory to begin your process. Choose any job you disliked. It may be your current job, your last job, or any job you had that was in some way significant to you. Fill out the left column only.

EXERCISE 3

Responses to My Current or Last Job

DISLIKES	LIKES

Now that you've tapped into your negative memories, you are ready to examine the things you enjoy, those elusive elements that are truly important to you. These are the enriching ingredients you value and want to ensure remain a part of your life.

Keeping each negative point in mind, ask yourself what you can learn from the information you've just recorded. Specifically, what does it tell you about you? If you could turn the negative around, what would the positive side be?

For example, if you wrote "bored" in the left column, in the right you might flip that over to say, "I need more intellectual stimulation." Or, "I like variety in my work." Or, "I thrive on physical activity." Only you know what the positive side should read. Only you can answer for you. Now, fill in the column on the right. Again, look for themes. Compare these themes with your earlier discoveries. Set this sheet aside; you will come back to it.

Illuminating the Real Me

Continuing Exercise 3 adds to the storehouse of information you are gathering about your values. The list you create on the right may be the characteristics or qualities of the job that will be "ideal" for you, under-standing, of course, that there are always compromises; the "perfect" job may not exist.

You will want to refer to the **MY LAST JOB** page at a later time, so keep the right-side **THINGS I VALUE** list handy for future reference. You may also wish to copy your summary of themes and threads under **THINGS I VALUE**. Indeed, it is a good idea to keep adding to the **THINGS I VALUE** list as you uncover the keys to your "ideal" job.

EXERCISE 3 cont.

Evaluating My Current or Last Job

THINGS I LIKED	THINGS I VALUE AND WANT TO KEEP

MAKING CONNECTIONS

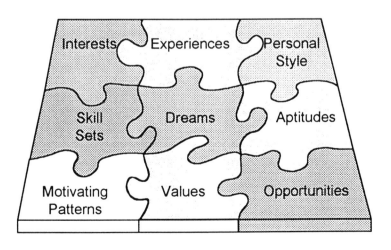

6

APPRECIATING PERSONAL WORTH

> We are the sum total of all the choices we have made.
> —Eleanor Roosevelt

Credit Where Credit Is Due

Experience demonstrates that there are essentially three kinds of people:

1. Those who make things happen

2. Those who watch things happen

3. Those who wonder "what happened?"

You are obviously the first kind of person and have decided to make things happen for yourself. As you read on, you will find that you are beginning to move towards your vision as you uncover your own truths, carve a new career path, and polish the skills you need in an increasingly competitive marketplace.

Good for you. You have started the difficult process of self-exploration, and you are to be congratulated. But stop! Give yourself a moment to put things in perspective.

It is often easy to see what we like best or value most about a friend, a co-worker, or a public figure. At this very moment, you could undoubtedly produce a glowing list of attributes of your favorite film star or statesman. But what we do for others, we usually forget to do for ourselves; what we see as laudable and admirable in others, we often fail to see in ourselves. While prospective employers value modesty, they also expect you to be candid about your strengths and weaknesses. You must be able to articulate your strengths in a way that is accurately descriptive.

Take a moment to give yourself a well-deserved pat on the back. No matter where you are in your life, no matter what your past history or fears of the future, you are a valuable person who deserves some recognition just for being the person you are. Complete the Performance Award below and give yourself credit!

EXERCISE 4

PERFORMANCE AWARD

What I like best about me is...

I am terrific at...

What I respect about me is...

And in addition...

7

STARTING OVER

No, you never get any fun out of things you haven't done.
—Ogden Nash

Letting Go of Myths

Parents, teachers, authority figures, and significant others often focus on negatives in their effort to provide us with direction or guidance. They mistakenly believe that by pointing out all your errors, you will learn to do things right; they think that by focusing on your weaknesses, you will build strengths; they are convinced that by reprimanding you, you will pull yourself together and shape up.

But intuitively or through personal experience, you know that focus on the negative creates doubt, flagging confidence, or worse.

A New Perspective

Because of today's changing workplace reality, you must take a new view of what lies ahead. It's time to:

Quit/Start

- thinking you know all you need to know/ a lifetime of learning

- depending on others for career guidance/taking responsibility for your own career

- depending on the "system" to move you ahead/looking for ways to move yourself within the system or outside of it

- bashing others/being accountable and proactive

- waiting for opportunities/building transferable skills

- counting on stability/recognizing change is constant

You want to target the positives in the next part of this self-discovery process. Begin with Exercise 5; it might be an eye-opener.

EXERCISE 5

Future Tense

Draw or describe a picture of what you might look like five years from now if things continue exactly as they are.

Future Perfect

Draw or describe a picture of what you might look like five years from now if things turn out *perfectly*.

Revisiting Goals and Dreams

Since charting a career path often begins with identifying your ideal or dream situation, a good next step is to create an ideal fantasy day for yourself.

EXERCISE 6

My Perfect Day

Imagine that this is a day in your life five years from now when everything is absolutely perfect.

☺ You wake up in the morning and open your eyes. What time is it?

_____

☺ Describe your environment. What do you see?

_____

_____

_____

☺ Are you alone or is somebody with you? If someone is there, who is it?

_____

☺ You get up and prepare for a day of work or leisure—your choice. How are you preparing? How are you dressing? What does your place look like? Is it in the country? City? Is it a house? Apartment?

_____

_____

_____

☺ Picture yourself going to work now. Where? How do you get there?

_____

_____

☺ Picture yourself in that place. What does it look like? Indoors? Outdoors? What are the details?

_____

_____

_____

☺ You are now greeting people at work. Describe them. What are their qualities? What do they care about?

_____

_____

_____

☺ What are you doing?

_____

_____

☺ At your place of work, you have co-workers. How do these people describe you?

_____

_____

_____

☺ What do you do for pleasure and leisure?

_____

Now that your fantasy is complete, summarize the key learning points for you. After you complete your summary, cross-check it with your list of **THINGS I VALUE.** Check for inconsistencies. Are the inconsistencies a result of personal growth and change in viewpoint, or do they reflect indecisiveness?

Personal Summary

8

21st Century Skills

People who feel good about themselves produce good results.
—Blanchard and Johnson

As the direction and methodology of business change, the skills required to meet the new demands are changing, too. In their book *Who's Going to Run General Motors?*, Kenneth Green and Daniel Seymour identify the following as skills we will need in the 21st century:

THE GREAT COMMUNICATOR—Communication Skills

- speak effectively to another individual

- write factual material clearly and concisely

- read with comprehension and speed

- question effectively

- write persuasively

- speak effectively to groups

- listen intently and objectively

- explain concepts well

- critique, edit, and proofread

- express feelings appropriately

THE TEAM PLAYER—Interpersonal Skills

- influence others

- negotiate and compromise

- withstand and resolve conflict

- understand the feelings of others

- encourage debate

- organize and delegate tasks

- motivate and develop other people

- appreciate and reward people's efforts

THE TECHNOLOGY MASTER—Technology Skills

- understand major hardware components

- use software packages

- use information to aid problem solving

- make graphic presentations

- access information from many sources

- transform raw data into useful information

- analyze data

- communicate using electronic means

THE PROBLEM SOLVER—Problem-Solving Skills

- define problems
- exhibit intellectual curiosity
- think abstractly and reflectively
- distinguish between fact and opinion
- propose and evaluate solutions
- possess an open, receptive mind
- defend a conclusion rationally
- bring reason to bear on a problem

THE AMBASSADOR—Multicultural Skills

- get along with other people
- accept other cultures
- speak other languages
- maintain openness to different ideas
- develop a global, not an ethnocentric, perspective
- understand cultural differences
- adjust to new conditions
- have no fixed prejudices
- feel curious about new situations
- understand the interdependence of nations in a global economy

THE CHANGE MAKER—Creativity and Innovation Skills

- face the unknown without fear
- develop a healthy, constructive nonconformity
- maintain a sense of imagination and curiosity
- assume moderate risks
- take responsibility for successes and failures
- tackle problems with unrepentant optimism
- develop a strong self-image
- accept change as a challenge
- overcome the fear of failure
- see things through

THE NEW LEADER—Leadership Skills

- articulate a vision
- show a willingness to accept responsibility
- understand followers and their needs
- demonstrate the need and drive to achieve
- motivate others
- accept and learn from criticism
- identify critical issues
- use tact, diplomacy, and discretion
- act decisively
- behave confidently and courageously

Creating Career Success

Be certain that the skills you are using daily are as well developed as they can be for the job you are required to do. Add to those skills a self-management attitude that drives you to:

- build on your skills

- develop new ones

- assess your strengths and weaknesses

- hear feedback as an opportunity to continue learning about yourself and your capabilities.

These are the determinant elements that create career success.

Since the percentage of people working at nontraditional jobs is increasing every day, as William Bridges says:

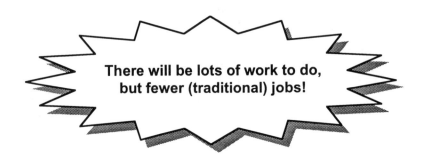

There will be lots of work to do, but fewer (traditional) jobs!

Increasing the Odds for Success

Think of examples of all the work that, as a direct consequence of our changing global outlook, has only recently been identified. For example, technological advances have resulted in traveling computer experts supporting the millions of personal computers now found in homes and offices; software design may once have been reserved for the computer giants, but swiftly changing interests have now created an entire cottage industry of software designers working on new and innovative projects, often for a niche market.

And that's not all. Authors can publish on an Internet, which did not exist a decade ago. A computer and modem make traveling to the office obsolete for a whole new sector of employees who telecommute. Technological advances offer sight to the visually impaired, locomotion for the physically impaired, and "visual telephones" for the hearing impaired. Professions, specialties, and expertise that did not exist a mere decade ago are suddenly required to deal with the interface between people and technology. But technology is not the only area worth considering. The list goes on and on.

For example, modular and moveable furniture has become the mainstay of office designers as companies flatten and the walls come tumbling down. Rent-a-grandma/pa is a new and thriving industry for healthy seniors. Changing demographics and limited governmental resources have generated profitable work for individuals who have found a new and cost-conscious way of serving the needs of the elderly, the impaired, the needy, or the young.

If the New Economy includes Global Communication, Technology, Quality-of-Life Focus, Personal Growth Issues, Changing Workplace, and Demographics, what new jobs are the result of these new features? What form do they take?

The key is to watch the trends so that you can develop ideas for work that needs doing—and then you can create it.

SECURITY
comes from your ability
to adapt to change

9

CHANGING COPING STRATEGIES

Tell me, and I'll forget. Show me, and I may remember. Involve me, and I'll understand.

—Native American saying

You may need to consider some new coping strategies for dealing with today's changing reality. The Engage program from Canada's Centre for Career Innovation in Alberta offers the following five truths to help you cope:

> **Recognize that Change is Constant**
>
> **Follow Your Heart**
>
> **Focus on the Journey**
>
> **Stay Learning**
>
> **Access Your Allies**

Debunking Myths

Given the work you have done thus far, you now know a little more about yourself and about the world as it changes and impacts your career goals. You are beginning the process of single-tracking your vision and your reality. But let's debunk a few myths before you move on.

MYTH: A CAREER IS SOMETHING YOU SELECT ONCE AND STICK WITH FOREVER.

REALITY: A career develops or evolves. In the end, your career may be light years away from your original goal and provide you with success and satisfaction you never imagined. Job change and even occupational change will be a part of our lives throughout our lives. The average North American currently changes jobs every three-and-a-half years. They change jobs because the world changes—and because they change.

MYTH: THERE IS A PERFECT FIT FOR ME SOMEWHERE—IF I COULD JUST FIND IT.

REALITY: There are probably many almost-perfect fits, but it is unlikely that any single one is perfect—there are always compromises. The trick in planning is to meet as many of your needs as possible.

Clarifying Your Vision

With information, you can begin to create a vision of what the world can be for you and what you can be in the world. It isn't enough to dream. And simply keeping busy is not the answer to getting where you want to go. You need a solid combination of motivation, dreams, and self-knowledge.

As Joel Barker tells us in *Paradigm Shifts,*

A VISION WITHOUT ACTION
IS A DREAM

ACTION WITHOUT A VISION
ONLY PASSES TIME

VISION WITH ACTION
CHANGES THE WORLD

You've started the process of career/life building, beginning with some reflection on who you are, examining the realities as they currently exist, and taking steps to explore what the future can hold for you. All of these are important pieces in the puzzle you must solve because you need both self-knowledge and a strong understanding of the world and of work in order to set goals for yourself.

To make meaningful choices, it is important that you take your long-term goals and dreams, put them into the context of your own reality, and mesh them with the reality of the 90s so that you can create a personal vision.

Your vision must be as clear and detailed as you can make it—and you must believe that it can happen. Only then can you translate your vision into goals that you write down, hang on the wall, and review frequently because those goals are crucial to your career path and key to your success.

VISION
If it isn't written,
it doesn't exist!

A goal casually set is freely abandoned at the first obstacle. You must really want it to achieve it. As Hopkins says, "a goal is a dream taken seriously."

At the moment, it is likely that you still have a blurry image of yourself and tunnel vision about the world—you see everything through your own cloudy microscope; we all do. But you need to take a broader view, and as you increase your understanding of where you fit and what will make you happy, your vision will become sharper. As you refine your vision, you will also refine your goals.

Keep in mind that as long as you are moving in the direction of your long-term goals, you are career building; all the little steps you take are concrete, positive actions towards your goals, and that is exactly what career building is all about.

Given your new understanding of the changing workplace and, indeed, the changing world, now may be a good time to clarify two terms.

A **job** is a position of paid employment with specific duties and responsibilities.

A **career** is the totality of work a person does in his or her lifetime. Other life roles, such as those related to family, community, leisure, and retirement, are included in a career.

Since a job has specific duties and responsibilities and a career is the totality of your work, everybody has jobs. And everybody has a career!

Now that you've done some self-examination, summarize the key learning points for you. After you complete your summary, you may wish to add to or revise your THINGS I VALUE list.

Personal Summary

10

Designing a Personal Blueprint for Success

The big trick is helping people to identify their own passions of what they want to do and where they want to do it.

—Richard Bolles

Career Carpentry

In this book we talk about career building or life planning. By that we mean the management of the many events and roles you experience that shape your career or your life. You can control some of these events and roles, such as your education or the relationships you choose; but others you can't control, such as the economy or technological change.

Career building and life planning is about you shaping your future opportunities—designing a personal blueprint for success. It requires the integration of new experiences, the visualization of short- and long-term goals, self-knowledge, understanding realities, and dreaming. It's about moving forward and stepping back to see where you are and where you want to go.

Career building is not *one big decision*. It's not about which occupation to choose or about choosing an occupation to last a lifetime. In today's roller-coaster environment, it is a mistake to lock into achieving X or Y because X or Y may no longer be there when you arrive. Career building requires flexibility and adaptability. Therefore, at least during this exploration phase, focus on the journey, not the destination.

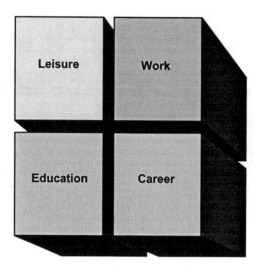

LIFE SATISFACTION

**CAREER/LIFE
PLANNING PROCESS**

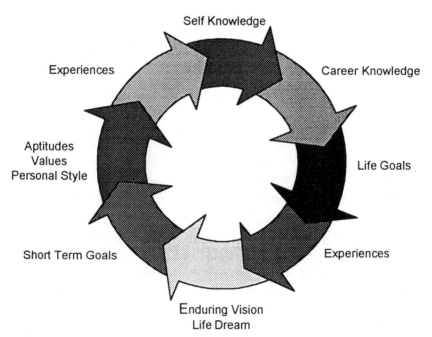

Self-Knowledge

You already know that self-knowledge requires an understanding of your interests, aptitudes, values, and personality. But you have to dig down to get at specifics. And before you do, let's define our terms.

Interests are topics or subjects about which you possess some knowledge and things you find fascinating or give meaning to what you so.

Aptitudes are endeavors for which you have a natural talent or the potential for being really good at.

Skills are the fulfillment of that potential or promise. For example, you may think you have a flair for taking photographs. That's an aptitude. You take a photography course and, with practice, you discover that you are the best in the class. That's a skill.

You may also have special **abilities** such as intelligence. We could say that **aptitude** is a finer breakdown of ability. Gardiner, a guru in the intelligence field, talks about seven kinds of natural intelligence:

- verbal or language ability
- numerical
- spatial
- kinesthetic
- musical
- inter-personal or getting along with others
- intra-personal or knowing oneself.

Values are concepts you can't touch but feel deeply. Some values are stable; others change with life experience.

Personality style or **temperament** is your natural or usual pattern of interacting with your environment. When people are not like you, when they have different personality styles or temperaments, that's when you feel like a fish out of water. When people are like you, when their styles or temperaments are similar to yours, that's when you feel most comfortable, relaxed, and at home.

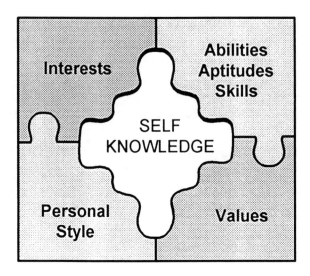

Only when you understand all of the above are you in a position to judge where you will best fit in, where you are most likely to succeed, and where your individual talents and skills are likely to be best appreciated and valued. An in-depth understanding of yourself increases your sense of being in charge of your future. Knowing yourself helps you to:

- determine the interests, skills, personality, and values that you have to offer a future employer

- identify the kind of work and type of environment in which you would be most satisfied and successful

- prepare for a successful job search by deciding what should be highlighted in your resume and how to answer questions in an employment interview.

So, what exactly are you looking for in your search for work? In terms of creating a career path, only when you know your values, interests, abilities, aptitudes, skills, and style can you make intelligent career or life-planning choices. Only then can you set appropriate and attainable goals, make solid plans, and develop suitable and applicable action steps.

To build a future where your personal needs are met, there are four areas believed to create a sense of satisfaction in life. These are relationships, education, leisure, and work.

Psychologists report that if one of these areas is not working well for you, you may feel stressed but still in control. If two or more of these areas is a problem for you, you may be feeling seriously tense and anxious. A truly fortunate person builds a future that includes attention to all four of these features.

No matter what your future holds, you need to:

- identify your marketable interests and special knowledge skills

- develop transferable skills

- be positive

- know yourself

- be prepared for change

- be a creative problem solver

- be prepared for a lifelong journey of learning.

Interests and Special Knowledge

You have done some preparatory work, and you have some of this information intuitively. But there are a number of worthwhile activities you can do to deepen your awareness.

The next section is primarily devoted to self-assessment tools that reveal your interests and special knowledge skills—the things you've learned to do that make you marketable. Skills are what you have to sell.

The purpose of doing these exercises is to generate a good deal of information before attempting to evaluate any of it. You generate this information using several methods, because any single strategy will not give you sufficient data for drawing conclusions. The more information you have, the more likely your self-assessment will be accurate. Remember to interpret the information in context. For example, the values questionnaire may help to isolate your values, but it does so without considering your personal strengths, skills, and so forth. So, choose only a few of these self-discovery exercises or do them all.

EXERCISE 7

Activity Diary

Since it is important to know how relationships, education, leisure, and work rank for you in terms of providing you with pleasure, fulfillment, contentment, or nourishment, you might want to start an activity journal.

Every day, for a time-limited period (you decide if it will be a day, a week, or two weeks), keep a record of your activities.

Your entries need not be lengthy or detailed because this is merely an assessment tool. But, for whatever period of time you choose, list *everything* you do from washing the dishes to taking the kids to the park, to walking the dog, to completing a report, or to playing cards with friends.

1. First, name the activity. Then, on a scale of 1 to 10 (1 = none at all, 10 = total), assign a "satisfaction" score. Below the score, list at least five reasons why you scored the activity the way you did.

For example, my activity was "Taking a Group French Lesson." I scored it a 7 because it was stimulating, intellectually challenging, social, slightly frustrating (I wanted to go faster), and tiring (because I am a day person, and it was a late class).

2. Attempt to explain each recorded activity in terms of an "identity statement." Answer the question: What does this activity say about who I am?

It generally takes a couple of weeks of recording your activities to isolate your themes. Review your diary, and you will quickly find recurring thoughts, words, images, likes, and dislikes. It is these recurring *themes*, written as identity statements, that tell you what you need to know; these themes are your drivers or motivators.

3. Do not attempt to evaluate or to make any judgments yet. Save the information you uncover and add it to what you learn in the other self-assessment exercises.

EXERCISE 8

Pictures to Go

There are still more ways to get in touch with your motivators, the things that, usually on a subliminal level, move you to action. A good exercise is to take five minutes every day and rifle through old magazines and newspapers. Tear out the items or pictures that "grab" you or "turn you on" and set them aside. Don't think about why you chose what you chose, just do it.

In about a month, set out all your pictures and take a good look at them. What are the themes? What is common to these pictures? What is it about them that "grabbed" you? It is very likely that your motivating patterns will be exposed in your collection of pictures.

The Ten Million Dollar Shopping List

So far, so good. Now, let's say you are financially independent, but you want to do something you love. You think you know what skills you have, but maybe you're still missing something important.

The marketplace reminds you every day that the ground is shifting beneath your feet, and you have finally come to the realization that change is constant; you have to be flexible enough to re-orient or re-invent yourself at any moment.

In all the exercises you have done thus far, you are attempting to pinpoint your interests and special knowledge so that you can create a vision for yourself based on the *inner you*. To do so, you must recognize that change will be ongoing.

Merle Shain, a well-respected author, writes about changing expectations in her books. She says, "You must decide if you want to act or react, deal your cards or play with a stacked deck. If you don't decide which way to play life, it always plays you."

Realizing that you are in the process of career building and life planning, it is important to understand that the key to satisfaction is following your heart, because your heart gives meaning to what you do. Your heart is your power source, and it provides the energy you need to navigate in the new world. You can clarify your vision by listening to the quiet voice within.

As you work through the next four exercises (The Shopping List, The Book Store, The Catalogue, and Taking the Stage), ask yourself what you know, what fascinates you, and about what you wish you knew more.

Start with the *Ten Million Dollar Shopping List*. This is a list you will keep and add to as you think of areas or opportunities you might like to know more about.

EXERCISE 9

My Shopping List

If I had $10 million and didn't have to work, how would I spend my time?

_____

_____

_____

_____

_____

_____

_____

EXERCISE 10

Visiting the Book Store

Let's continue to explore your special knowledge and interests. Here is another activity to try. If you come up with something new, add it to your shopping list.

SPECIAL KNOWLEDGE BOOK STORE

Imagine you have all the time in the world to browse through a book store. It is a wonderful book store with books on every topic imaginable.

List the *subjects* of the books that interest you (e.g., marketing, women, science fiction, gardening).

_____

_____

_____

EXERCISE 11

Checking the Catalogues

You are flipping through the pages of an enormous mail order catalogue, the sort of catalogue where you find anything and everything. On which pages do you spend more time?

Again, if you come up with something new, add it to your shopping list (e.g., animals, gardening tools, photography equipment).

SPECIAL KNOWLEDGE THE MAIL ORDER CATALOGUE

_____

_____

EXERCISE 12

Taking the Stage

You are an expert on something or want to be. Imagine that you are about to give a speech about this topic, and you are not the least bit nervous because you have become a real authority; you've learned more about the topic than almost anyone else in the world. What is the topic?

Again, if you come up with something new, add it to your shopping list (e.g., hair styles, making travel plans, canoeing).

SPECIAL KNOWLEDGE SPEECH

_____

_____

EXERCISE 13

Discovery Summary

1. To your "Ten Million Dollar Shopping List" add any activities you uncovered in the book store, catalogue, or speech exercise that you might be interested in actually pursuing.

2. On a blank piece of paper, make a list of all of your interests or special knowledge. Make sure that each item that you list is a noun, a subject, a topic, a booklet in your head, or something you could give a talk about or would like to learn about. It could be plants, mechanics, or a history of America but should not be names of occupations.

3. Narrow down your list by:

    a. eliminating any item you do not like very much

    b. combining similar or related items (e.g., athletics and sports)

c. eliminating any that you are certain you want to do in your leisure, not in your work.

4. Prioritize below your top 10 items of interest using number one as your favorite interest.

MY FAVORITE INTERESTS/SPECIAL KNOWLEDGE

1.

2.

3.

4.

5.

6.

7.

8.

9.

10.

ASSESSING MY WORLD

EXERCISE 14

Personal Inventory

Use a colored pen or crayon for each list and circle the words that
fit you. Have another color pen ready for friendly feedback.

Summary

1. On a blank sheet of paper, make a list of all of your traits
   under the headings:

   - INTERESTS (some of these are special knowledge
     skills that relate to a particular job or subject matter)

   - APTITUDES AND SKILLS (these are transferable
     skills)

   - VALUES

   - PERSONAL STYLE

2. Narrow down your list by:

    a. eliminating any traits that you believe are not an important part of your personality

    b. eliminating any traits you possess but do not enjoy.

3. Now, you need friendly feedback. Ask a trustworthy friend, partner, or mentor to read the personal inventory list, circle the words they believe apply to you, and give you feedback based on their assessment of how they see you. Compare the other person's list to yours using the Friendly Feedback Sheet.

EXERCISE 15

Friendly Feedback

From what I see, and from my experience with you, I believe:

You are interested in _____

You are especially skilled at _____

Your values include _____

Your greatest strengths and most marketable skills are

_____

Friendly Feedback Phase II
(This section will be filled out later.)

What are my best personality traits?

What are my personality weaknesses?

What skills do you see that you believe are most marketable?

What do you think I don't know about myself and should be aware of?

What do you think is important to me in my work?

INTERESTS/ SP. KNOWLEDGE	APTITUDES & SKILLS	VALUES	PERSONAL STYLE
adventure			academic
advocacy			accurate
animals			active
art/design			adaptive/flexible
astronomy			adventurous
budgets	administrating	accuracy	ambitious
business/marketing	advising	achievement	analytical
cars	analyzing	action	calm
coaching	budgeting	challenge	caring
computers	competing	competence	cheerful/optimistic
crafts	computing numbers	competition	competitive
drama/acting	constructing	cooperation	confident
education	consulting	courage	conservative
electronics	creating	creativity	cooperative
environment	delegating	dignity/respect	creative
family	designing	diligence	curious
fix things/tools	emergency	efficiency	dependable
food/nutrition	response	excitement	detail-oriented
graphic design	harmony	fairness	dignified
health	helping	fitness	direct
helping	inventing	friends	easy-going
ideas	listening	harmony	energetic/
languages	maintaining/	home/family	enthusiastic
law	managing	independence	entertaining/
layout	marketing	intelligence/	humorous
machines	motivating	education	fair
math	observing	justice	formal
medicine	organizing details	leadership	friendly
music	performing	logic/order	generous
nature/outdoors	persuading	modesty	helpful
paint/draw	physical	money	impatient
photography	coordination	play	impulsive
politics	problem solving	privacy	independent
psychology	public speaking	recognition	inquiring
relationship	repairing	resourcefulness	intellectual
sales	researching	security	logical
science	resolving	trust	organized
sewing	selling	truth	persistent
sports	synthesizing	variety	polite
teaching/training	teaching		practical/sensible
technology	teamwork		sensitive
travel	using tools		sincere
writing	writing/editing		versatile

PERSONAL INVENTORY

EXERCISE 16

Clustering Skills

After all the work you have done, you must begin to organize the information you have gathered. Start by clustering your skills (i.e., putting things together that are closely related).

Using the skills you identified in the preceding exercises and the information on your Friendly Feedback Sheet, cluster your skills and attributes into related groups under the headings on the Skills Cluster List that follows. (Yes, some skills will be repeated under more than one heading.)

SKILLS CLUSTER LIST

Management   Administrative   Counseling/Advocacy
_____   _____   _____
_____   _____   _____

Leadership   Physical Activity   Sales/Promotion
_____   _____   _____
_____   _____   _____

Teaching/Training   Manual Skills   Research/Analysis
_____   _____   _____
_____   _____   _____

Oral Communication   Interpersonal Skills   Academic/Education
_____   _____   _____
_____   _____   _____

Written Communication   Artistic Skills   Other
_____   _____   _____
_____   _____   _____

Creative Skills   Undeveloped Skills
_____   _____
_____   _____

Summing Up Motivated Skills

Everyone has a variety of skills, aptitudes, and special knowledge, but not all the skills we use please or motivate us. It is the motivated skills, a blend of interests and skills, that create real satisfaction.

If the key to contentment is to focus on the journey, remember that:

- you need a general direction for the future, not a specific target

- your goals must be flexible

- every decision is a career decision

- the journey must be meaningful.

EXERCISE 17

Moving Forward

1. On a blank sheet of paper, make a list of your most motivated skills, that is, those you most enjoy using. Take these from all the work you have done thus far, such as your diary, pictures, and/or skills cluster list.

2. Narrow down your list by:

   a. eliminating any skill you would not love to use in a work situation

   b. grouping skills that are similar

   c. eliminating a skill you use a lot but don't enjoy using

3. List your 10 most motivated skills on the next page.

4. Flesh out your top 10 skills by adding an object or thing, information or ideas, or people. For example, you might have written "organizing" as a motivating skill (organizing what?).

- information on a computer?

- people—on a work team?

- nuts and bolts on a work bench?

MY MOST IMPORTANT MOTIVATED SKILLS

	SKILLS	OBJECT (Purpose—what, with whom?)
Example:	writing	for the company newsletter • interviews • gathering and analyzing new info
1.		
2.		
3.		
4.		
5.		
6.		
7.		
8.		
9.		
10.		

Identifying Aptitudes and Transferable Skills

We all have skills that we have used to accomplish things and that are transferable to other areas of work and life.

1. Think of a time in your life when you did something:

    a. that gave you a sense of achievement;

    b. that made you feel good because you had accomplished something;

    c. when you were truly enjoying yourself.

2. Identify the skills you used to do the job.

Applying the Information

As the song says, "you've looked at life from both sides now." So, what will you do with all this information? Begin looking for ways to apply it to your career plan by filling in the Information Applications Sheet below.

EXERCISE 18

Information Applications

Needs/Values	Short-Term Goals	Long-Term Goals	Financial Needs
_____	_____	_____	_____
_____	_____	_____	_____
Transferable Skills	Special Knowledge	Interests	Personality Strengths
_____	_____	_____	_____
_____	_____	_____	_____

An example of how one might fill out the **Information Applications** form appears on the next page. Of course, yours will be different, but you get the idea.

SAMPLE INFORMATION APPLICATIONS

Needs/Values	Short-Term Goals	Long-Term Goals	Financial Needs
•independence	•ask for raise	•home-based	•retirement plan
•creativity	•take budgeting	business	•renegotiate
•travel	course	•financial stability	mortgage
•more family time	•volunteer for Big Brothers	•cruise with Wendy	•forced savings

Transferable Skills	Special Knowledge	Interests	Personality Strengths
•sales	•automotive	•cars	•creative
•inter-personal	•electronics	•fixing things	•risk-taking
•manual		•travel	•reliable
•creativity			

IDENTIFYING VALUES

Identifying Work Values

In the previous exercises, you began the process of single tracking your life values with your work goals. Clarifying personal values will help to pinpoint the work values you seek. Work values are those enduring aspects of work that are regarded as important sources of satisfaction.

EXERCISE 19

The following list describes a wide variety of satisfactions that people obtain from their jobs. Look at the definitions of these various satisfactions and, using the scale below, rate the degree of importance that you would assign to each for yourself.

1 = Not important at all

2 = Not very important

3 = Reasonably important

4 = Very important in my choice of career

VALUES	RATING 1–4
ACHIEVEMENT: Work that offers the opportunity to excel.	
ADVANCEMENT: Work that offers opportunities for development and promotion.	
AESTHETICS: Work that provides the opportunity to study or create beauty.	
APPROVAL: Work that provides opportunity for positive feedback from others.	
BALANCE: Work that offers an opportunity to balance task and people.	
CHALLENGE: Work that offers an intellectual or physical challenge.	
CHANGE: Work that requires flexibility and demands frequent change in duties or responsibilities.	
COACHING and COUNSELING: Work that provides opportunity for guiding others.	
COMPETENCY: Work that promotes doing what you do well.	
COMPETITION: Work that pits one's skills or talents against others'.	
COOPERATION: Activities that depend on a high degree of cooperation.	
CREATIVITY: Work that promotes pursuing new ideas, innovative concepts, originality, etc.	
DECISION MAKING: Work that confers the power to decide direction, practices, policies, etc.	
EXCITEMENT and RISK TAKING: Work that provides a high degree of risk or frequent excitement.	
FRIENDSHIP: Work that provides opportunity for developing close and meaningful relationships.	
INDEPENDENCE: Work that permits a high degree of autonomy and self-reliance.	
INFLUENCE: Work that provides power and opportunity to change attitudes or opinions.	
KNOWLEDGE: Work that encourages the pursuit of knowledge, truth, and understanding.	
NURTURING: Work that requires helping others directly.	
ORDER: Work that permits attention to process; work that fits into a hierarchy.	
PERFECTIONISM: Work that encourages a high degree of attention to detail.	
POWER and AUTHORITY: Work that permits me to control the activities or the fate of others.	
PROBLEM-SOLVING: Work that promotes creating alternatives and new solutions to problems.	
PROFIT/GAIN: Work that results in accumulating large amounts of money or other material gain.	
RECOGNITION: Work that promotes public notice of my accomplishments.	
RELATIONSHIPS: Work that results in developing close personal relationships.	
RESULTS ORIENTATION: Activities that produce quantifiable or qualifiable results or visible end products.	
SECURITY: Work that offers high assurance of job stability and reasonable financial reward.	
SELF-EXPRESSION: Work that allows me to express who I am through what I do.	
SOCIAL CONSCIENCE: Work that contributes to a better world.	
STABILITY and PREDICTABILITY: Work that includes a predictable routine and job duties.	
STATUS: Work that provides the opportunity to be acknowledged as an "expert" in my field.	
TASK ORIENTATION: Work that is primarily task, not people, oriented.	
TEAMWORK: Work that provides an opportunity to develop close relationships with a group; working as part of a team.	
WISDOM: Work that provides opportunity for maturation and the development of acumen, knowledge, and insight.	
OTHERS:	

1. List all the values you scored at 4.

    _____

    _____

    _____

    _____

    _____

    _____

    _____

    _____

    _____

2. Prioritize the above list.

    _____

    _____

    _____

    _____

    _____

    _____

    _____

    _____

    _____

3. Return to the trustworthy friend who filled out your Friendly
    Feedback Sheet and ask for additional feedback by having
    them answer the following questions:

    •   What are my best personality traits?

    •   What are my personality weaknesses?

    •   What skills do you see that you believe are most
        marketable?

    •   What do you think I don't know about myself and
        should be aware of?

    •   What do you think is important to me in my work?

4. Review and adjust your Skills Cluster List.

13

CAREER KNOWLEDGE

In addition to self-awareness, imagination and conscience, it is the fourth human endowment—independent will—that really makes effective self-management possible.

—Stephen R. Covey

The New Organization

The New Organization has been restructured to achieve:

- flexibility and adaptability for quick response to marketplace demands

- productivity and efficiency

- cost effectiveness.

The New Organization includes:

1. Core employees or partners

   - who are fully employed

   - who define the organization's core competence

   - who decide what is unique or distinct about the organization

- who plan strategy and set goals

- who define the vision.

2. Customers and clients who do work that used to be done by employees (e.g., ATMs, self-serve gas stations, Ikea).

3. Vendors and sub-contractors

- who receive fees for results rather than salary for time

- who contract for jobs, products, and services.

4. Temporary or term employees

- who come and go as needed

- who work on project-driven jobs

- who work temporarily on a specific project.

Alternative Workstyles

As companies reorganize and The New Organization restructures and reorganizes itself, the natural aftermath is for employees to consider alternative workstyles.

As you examine the continuum from full employment (where almost every aspect of the job is understood, where there is little in the way of surprise, and where there is a great deal of security) through to entrepreneurship (where flexibility, risk-taking, and comfort with the unknown are essential ingredients), you can identify that point on the continuum where your personal needs are best met.

Single Tracking

So far, so good. You have completed the Personal Inventory and Work Values Questionnaire. You've written a diary, visited a hypothetical book store, given an imaginary speech, and are in the process of collecting pictures. And while you now know your motivated skills,

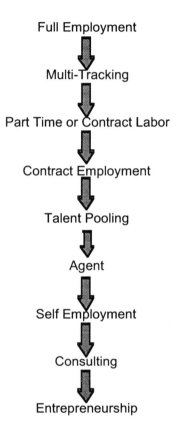

ALTERNATIVE WORK STYLES

Full Employment

Multi-Tracking

Part Time or Contract Labor

Contract Employment

Talent Pooling

Agent

Self Employment

Consulting

Entrepreneurship

transferrable skills, and values, while you've looked at The New Organization and alternative workstyles, you may still be uncertain of exactly where you fit—how to find work that is on the same track as your personality. Why not try The Cosmic Category Test?

"Know thyself." These words, attributed to Socrates, were inscribed on the Temple of Delphi over 2,000 years ago. The idea that we should learn all we can about ourselves has stood the test of time; our quest towards self-discovery continues today, although it is perhaps more difficult in our sophisticated world. Knowing who you are *now* is the first and most important step in deciding where you belong in the *future*. Years of research have established that the information required to encourage insight, personal growth, and self-esteem is contained within our own thoughts. If people are provided with accurate information about the way they *think*, they can make intelligent decisions and increase their overall effectiveness.

Carl Jung speaks of archetypes as expressions of the structure of the human psyche. He suggests that universally, there are repetitive motifs or personality types. There are a number of well-known personality tests that attempt to identify personality type. Some are rather simple, others very complicated. But they are all tools for increasing self-knowledge.

Obviously, you need the right tools to do anything well. Just as discovering the precise meaning of a word is easy when you refer to a dictionary, designing a career path is easier when you have suitable information to assist you.

THE COSMIC CATEGORY TEST

The **Cosmic Category Test** is simply another tool. It is a quick and easy test designed to provide you with information about your core personality style so that you know your natural behavioral patterns and specific personality strengths. This, in addition to the work you have already done, should nail it all down for you—who you are and what pleases, nourishes, or satisfies you. People are born with a genetic mix that is uniquely their own—unlike any other person in the world. Your genetic package predisposes you to behave or to think in a particular way, that is, to fit into an identifiable personality category. Of course, your personality will be shaped by your experiences, your caregivers, your education, and your circumstances. Still, you do come into the world with a tendency towards a personality style.

Obviously, personality is a complex issue—you always knew that, and you were reminded of it when you earlier compared your own notes to the feedback of your friend, partner, or mentor. While sociologists and psychologists have a vast array of tests and strategies to figure out the complexities of character or temperament, it has long been believed that there are essentially four core styles.

If you are wondering why you should bother with this test, there are a number of good reasons. Do it to:

☺ clarify your understanding of your natural style

☺ find work that "fits"

☺ present your attributes where you know the qualities you possess are respected and valued

☺ feel content with the work you find

☺ set realistic goals on the basis of your values and objectives

☺ feel valued

☺ improve relationships

☺ be happy with your self-image

☺ create a fuller, more rewarding life.

Warning

Personality or aptitude tests are merely indicators and should not be considered the final word. A single test provides only a piece of the puzzle, not the whole picture. Use this test, or any similar test, to confirm what you already suspect from your self-assessment work. Should you want to try other well-tested instruments and compare results, you might consider the Myers-Briggs Type Indicator® and the Strong Interest Inventory™.

COSMIC CATEGORY TEST

1. Read and Rank Categories

Each of the four descriptive categories has distinguishing character-istics. Read them carefully and rank them below from 4 (most like me) down to 1 (least like me). Transfer your **descriptive total** score to the Tally Sheet at the end of the test.

poonams

DESCRIPTIVE TOTAL

2 STAR   _____

3 METEOR   _____

3 SUN   _____

4 PLANET   _____

12

Star

Your primary driver is achievement.

You are a high performer and focus on excellence and goal achievement. You enjoy a good balance between task and people. Often analytical, sometimes overly critical and competitive, you are an independent thinker with a tendency to be nonconformist and intellectually curious. Creative, secure, and spirited, you believe that your personal effort can make a difference.

You enjoy having information and tackling complex issues, and as a self-confident, innovative individual, you generally want independence from authority. You prefer to set your own goals, and as an enthusiastic activist, you are willing to take moderate risks to produce results. Sometimes argumentative, you are a change maker and a visionary who searches for things that need doing and creative solutions for doing them.

As a Star, you are self-directed and primarily motivated by your own beliefs and values. You are a skilled problem solver and thrive on challenge. You focus on success and are a "high performer."

Meteor

Your primary driver is self-actualization.

You are a fun-loving, uninhibited, optimistic doer who needs the freedom to explore opportunities and challenge. You enjoy stretch goals and self-development. Generous and charming, you are committed to your beliefs and tend to focus on personal growth and development. You enjoy hands-on experience and are inclined to pursue change and variety.

Good in a crisis, you are responsible, confident, relaxed, and driven to accomplish the goals you set. While you are perceptive and understanding, your strength is in your flexibility, adaptability, and joyful approach to life. Sometimes overly competitive, you are confident, eager, and often impatient. Others may admire you or envy you, but they are rarely neutral to you.

As a Meteor, you tend to be a risk taker and are a natural entrepreneur. You may be spontaneous and somewhat impulsive, but still you are realistic in that you accept the cards you are dealt and enjoy the moment, always striving to get the most out of every life experience.

Sun

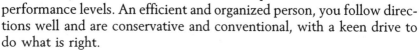

Your primary driver is humanism.

You are super-dependable, loyal, punctual, decisive, sensible, and people-centered, qualities that allow you to achieve and maintain superior performance levels. An efficient and organized person, you follow directions well and are conservative and conventional, with a keen drive to do what is right.

While socially responsible and focused on developing, helping, and teaching others, you like people and tend to accept them unconditionally. Your strong moral code promotes some dependence, and while you do not often resist authority, you do resist change. People who know you well admire your depth of passion and commitment; others may consider you rather uninteresting.

As a Sun, you are conscientious and caring. You are concerned about what other people think and are driven by a strong moral imperative to do what is right. Your strength is in your ability to establish and maintain warm and supportive relationships. You have the ability to inspire and motivate others and are unfailingly optimistic about what people can accomplish.

Planet

Your primary driver is relationships.

You are supportive, nurturing, reliable, cooperative, empathetic, and a strong team player. With a focus on affiliation, you regard people as more important than things and develop strong and meaningful relationships with many friends. Somewhat mysterious, you are sensual, romantic, and very sensitive to conflict, which you dislike. You enjoy networking and are a good friend and considerate lover.

Having highly developed interpersonal skills, you strive to meet the needs of others while continuing to develop yourself and deepen your understanding of your own role and purpose. You are also imaginative, spiritual, and idealistic, with a strong motivation to stick to core values.

As a Planet, your strength is in your ability to motivate others and to understand that they, like you, need understanding, encouragement, and recognition.

2. Choose a Role Model

Choose a person, living or dead, real or fictional, whose character and temperament you most admire. Knowing what you now know about Cosmic Categories, rank that person from 4 (most like that person) to 1 (least like that person). _Plant_

STAR...METEOR...SUN...PLANET...

3. Read the Word Clusters

Read each cluster of words and rank the cluster from 4 (most like me) down to 1 (least like me).

SCORE

____ 1.   questioning, secure, goal-oriented, ambitious 4

____ 2.   respected, witty, fun-loving, confident 4

____ 3.   cooperative, warm, genuine, intuitive 4

____ 4.   loyal, humanistic, stable, follow rules 3

____ 5.   encouraging, trusted, reliable, concrete 3

____ 6.   sensitive, authentic, well-liked, emotional 4

____ 7.   entertaining, good leader, principled, like variety 4

____ 8.   fair, independent-thinker, creative, results-oriented 3

___ 9.   open, spontaneous, competitive, enthusiastic 2

___ 10.   imaginative, tactful, caring, self-searching 3

___ 11.   organized, fair, helpful, encouraging 4

___ 12.   enjoy challenge, visionary, analytical, conceptual 3

___ 13.   creative thinker, optimistic, versatile, adventurous 4

___ 14.   direct, calm, nonconformist, innovative 2

___ 15.   good teacher, methodical, loyal, conservative 3

___ 16.   spiritual, empathetic, accept change, like harmony 3

___ 17.   dependable, compassionate, cooperative, conventional 4

___ 18.   intellectual, achieving, respected, enjoy challenge 4

___ 19.   good communicator, risk taker, independent, 4
          charming

___ 20.   nurturing, relaxed, idealistic, flexible 4

___ 21.   flexible, impatient, self-empowered, happy 4

___ 22.   dedicated, reliable, dependent, considerate 4

___ 23.   poetic, inclusive, enthusiastic, avoid conflict 3

___ 24.   change agent, logical, well-liked, risk taker 3

___ 25.   generous, good listener, empowering, compliant 2

___ 26.   lifelong learner, self-directed, competitive, 3
          initiator

___ 27.   exciting, doer, in touch with self, change agent 3

___ 28.   concerned, down-to-earth, risk-averse, humanistic

___ 29.   I value security, tradition, cooperation, friendships

___ 30.   I value freedom, variety, self-actualization, stimulation

___ 31.   I value logic, intelligence, achievement, independence

___ 32.   I value—harmony, justice, individuality, family and friends

4. Score

Transfer your scores to the tally sheet below.

TALLY SHEET

STAR

1...8...12...14...18...24...26...31...   TOTAL.....

+ DESCRIPTIVE TOTAL... + ROLE MODEL TOTAL...   FINAL TOTAL...

METEOR

2...7...9...13...19...21...27...30...   TOTAL.....

+ DESCRIPTIVE TOTAL... + ROLE MODEL TOTAL...   FINAL TOTAL...

SUN

4...5...11...15...17...22...25...29...   TOTAL.....

+ DESCRIPTIVE TOTAL... + ROLE MODEL TOTAL...   FINAL TOTAL...

PLANET

3...6...10...16...20...23...28...32...   TOTAL.....

+ DESCRIPTIVE TOTAL... + ROLE MODEL TOTAL...   FINAL TOTAL...

Analysis of Results

Your primary Cosmic Category is the one in which you scored highest. Finding work in an environment that values and supports your primary style is believed to be the least stressful. Your secondary Cosmic Category is the one in which you scored next highest. Working in an environment that values and supports your secondary style is likely to be very comfortable. Your third highest score is your tertiary category. Unless your top three scores are very close, working in an environment that primarily values your tertiary style is likely to provoke an element of stress.

In looking for work that will satisfy and nourish you, begin your search among the occupations that are most likely to be of interest to your Cosmic Category. If you have two or three scores that are very close, search all the occupations that are most likely to be of interest to both your primary and secondary categories. Brainstorm occupations that seem to be missing from the list but which you believe would fit the category.

Next Step

Go back to your Ten Million Dollar Shopping List. Knowing what you now know about yourself and scanning the occupations list that fits most closely with your style, add a section to your Shopping List page: Occupations to Explore.

STAR OCCUPATIONS	METEOR OCCUPATIONS	SUN OCCUPATIONS	PLANET OCCUPATIONS
accountant/actuary	actor/musician	accountant/auditor	actor
advertising executive	advertising executive	air traffic controller	advertising specialist
anthropology	animal trainer	attorney/paralegal	career counselor
architecture	architect	auto mechanic	child care worker
astronaut	artist/art therapist	banker/teller	customer service rep
athlete	athlete	bookkeeper	ergonomics specialist
attorney/judge	bartender	carpenter	esthetition
banker	broadcaster/	cashier	flight attendant
biological technician	comedian	child care worker	guidance counselor
biomedical engineer	carpenter	claims clerk	hair stylist
chemist	child care worker	coach	head hunter/recruiter
chiropractor	cosmetologist	computer	hospital administrator
computer sciences	dance teacher	programmer	human resources
criminologist	designer—any field	computer repair	specialist
dental assistant	disc jockey	correctional	interior designer
editor/journalist	entrepreneur	services officer	manager/supervisor
electrician	fire fighter	court reporter	mediator
embalmer	flight attendant	curator	motivational speaker
engineer	fund raiser	data entry person	nurse
environmentalist	gardener	dentist/assistant	occupational
film technician	human resources	editor	therapist
investment banker	specialist	executive assistant	paramedic
investment	labor specialist	financial planner	poet
counselor	management	hospital	psychologist
legal assistant	consultant	administrator	real estate agent
management	marketing specialist	insurance agent	receptionist
consultant	mediator	judge	recreation therapist
manufacturer	medical illustrator	lab technician	recruiter
mortgage broker	midwife	librarian	rehabilitation
occupational	occupational	manager/supervisor	counselor
therapist	therapist	payroll clerk	religious leader
orthodontist	paramedic	personnel specialist	sales person
photographer	party coordinator	physical therapist	social worker
physician	phys-ed teacher	physician/nurse	team leader
physicist	physician/assistant	postal worker	therapist
podiatrist	politician	public administrator	tour guide
pollster	producer	radiologist/technician	travel agent
prosthetics designer	public speaker	real estate agent	writer
re-engineering	real estate agent	receptionist	
consultant	sales person	research assistant	
researcher	social worker	sales person	
stock broker	stock broker	school administrator	
systems engineer	systems designer	social worker	
technical writer	training and devel-	teacher	
university professor	opment specialist	telephone operator	
urban planner	truck driver	trades person	
veterinarian	writer	veterinary assistant	

15

PIECING THE PUZZLE TOGETHER

> Things which matter most should never be at the mercy of things which matter least.
>
> —Goethe

Finding the Missing Pieces

In all the work you've just done, you have been looking at what is. You also want to look at what could be...

...if you developed a skill you wish you had.

...if you learned more about the things that intrigue you.

...if you identified the missing pieces.

To find the missing pieces, ask yourself:

- Am I using my favorite skills in my current job?

- Are there ways in which I could enrich my current job using more of my favorite skills?

- Are there skills I should develop to prepare for my next career move?

Summary

1. Return to your Skills Cluster List and under "Undeveloped Skills," add any skills you very much enjoy using but which you know are undeveloped.

2. Make a list of all the skills you need to learn, develop, or improve.

3. Refer to the pages on 21st Century Skills to add to your skills cluster, shopping, or exploration lists.

4. Using career information resources, research one occupation from your Explore List to learn what skills are required for success in this occupation. List them on the **Interesting Occupations Form** that follows the format for 21st Century Skills in Chapter 8.

5. Use the Interesting Occupations Form as a tool to identify new occupations and jobs you want to consider. It will:

    *   generate a list of options that build on your favorite skills

    *   be a starter kit for:

        —the job hunt

        —functional resumes

        —information and job interviews.

EXERCISE 20

Interesting Occupations Form

Name of Occupation	Skills Required	I Have This Skill	I Need to Develop This Skill

A PERSONAL VISION: FOLLOW YOUR BLISS

Freedom is what you do with what's been done to you.
—Jean-Paul Sartre

Defining Your Vision

Most organizations have a Vision Statement written on the wall. It helps them focus on what is really important; a personal Vision Statement does precisely the same thing.

Begin this exercise by looking inward. For the moment, forget about the job hunt, finances, and competencies. What would you really like to do with your time? You may have thought often about things like starting a fitness program or getting enough money to travel more often. But think deeper. Think about the inner you—who you are and what you expect in life.

Because you are asked to create a symbol to represent your thoughts —a visual representation of abstract concepts—this activity may stir you in ways the preceding ones didn't. The next two pages will help you to discover some of the secrets you may be keeping, even from yourself.

EXERCISE 21

Personal Visioning

Answer the following questions:

1. What would I like my epitaph to say?

2. What has been a deep and meaningful learning experience in my life?

3. What characteristics or traits do I want to improve?

4. What characteristics or traits do I like best about myself?

5. What am I best at?

6. What do I want to accomplish in my life?

7. What do I need to enrich my life?

8. What are my most important life goals?

9. Who am I?

10. What person, living or dead, would I most wish to be like?

Keeping your answers in mind, create a symbol on the next page for each of the following: work, family, leisure, and friends. Choose symbols that represent your dreams and goals to create a symbolic picture of the real you.

My Vision

17

TAKING THE LEAP

Find yourself and be yourself. Remember, there is no one else on earth like you.
—Dale Carnegie

Clarifying the Context

Either you decided long ago to make a change, or it was decided for you. Whichever it was, you don't have to take the leap without a net. The best net is comprised of a solid base of information and understanding.

As you have worked through the process gaining self-knowledge and career knowledge, you have tried to keep all your discoveries within the context of work. Debarah H. Wilson, a career transition specialist in Menlo Park, California (Careerpro2@aol.com and on the Net at http://amsquare.com/amerway/career.html), suggests that as you turn from looking in to looking out, as you get ready to leap into the marketplace, keep your potential employer in mind. According to Wilson:

In order for you to successfully market yourself, you should understand what your strengths are and how they will benefit a prospective employer. In today's market employers want to know how you can "save them money," increase their "profitability," and "fit" within the company culture. Here are a few of the areas you should evaluate:

- Related work history

- Relevant career progression

- Successful work history

- Longevity

- Communications ability—verbal, written, and presentation

- Assertiveness and leadership ability

- Good attitude and flexibility

- Problem solver and troubleshooter

- Good interpersonal skills, able to work with all levels

- Basic education, related or advanced

- Understanding of company culture

- Ability to assert control

At the core of the career-building process is your ability to assert control over your life and your future. Paul Stevens of The Centre for Worklife Counselling in Sydney, Australia (http://www.ozemail.com.au/%7Eworklife/control.html) is a recipient of the Resource Award from the International Career Planning and Adult Development Network. The author of *Beating Job Burnout: Stop Postponing the Rest of Your Life* and literally (no joke) dozens of other books on career transitions and life journeys, Stevens has created a valuable checklist he suggests you refer to regularly. While some of the items relate specifically to individuals currently working, Stevens' list is an excellent summary of the work you have done thus far and is reprinted here with permission.

Asserting Control Over Your Career

1. My first responsibility is to be true to myself—everything I do is a choice.

2. It's O.K. to be apprehensive about change.

3. I am most likely to be effective for my employer's benefit—and mine—if I focus on a job and career direction that fits my values and preferred skills.

4. I will welcome "mistakes" as opportunities for learning and improving.

5. No career action step will be resolved without deep consideration of the factors affecting my living outside work.

6. I will present a Career Action Step proposal at work, which identifies activities and responsibilities I would prefer to have more of in current and future work.

7. While I will be guided by a career action step plan, I will remain open for adjustment and unexpected opportunity.

8. I will weather change well by having a "safety net" of awareness of my preferred skills, career values, primary wants, and contribution value to my employer's customers.

9. I will not be able to achieve my career goals alone and will actively seek the support of others.

10. The meaning of success for me will alter as I journey through living—I will take care to redefine myself at regular intervals.

Tackling Major Issues

In pursuit of your goals, there is no doubt that obstacles, small or large, will plant themselves in your path without so much as an invitation. You may find that your family is just not as supportive as you had hoped or that financial considerations seem to have you glued to a dead-end job. Sandy McMillan of Career Solutions in the United Kingdom asks, "What will be different in your chosen future?"

McMillan, an international authority on career building, has written a series of worksheets and workbooks to help people move forward. Worksheet Two© is excellent for helping you to consider your options when you are dissatisfied and for taking a strategic approach to tackling a major issue. For more about Career Solutions, find them on the Net at http://w3.win-uk.net/ppp/career.

McMillan's Worksheet Two© is reprinted here with permission.

Career Solutions Worksheet Two©

If something's seriously wrong, you have seven possible strategies:

1. **Change the situation.**

Change things physically—equipment, processes, or procedures. This is a very logical approach that can be effective. However, it may not work if people have strong feelings about what's happening.

2. **Change other people.**

Influence the key people in the situation to behave in a different way. This implies learning skills and tactics to persuade other people.

3. **Leave the situation.**

Move on from the unsatisfactory situation—get yourself promoted? Make sure that you go to something better, not just away from something you don't like.

4. Change yourself.

Learn how to behave in a way that improves the situation. Again, you'll need to learn some new skills and techniques.

5. Change how you see it.

Find a new way to see the situation so that it no longer seems wrong. Though this appears, at first sight, to be impossible, it can work well. People can, and do, change their attitudes—it doesn't usually happen overnight, but it does happen.

6. Put up with it.

Hope that things will improve if you give them enough time. If you don't like confrontations or are not feeling very confident, then this is a tempting strategy, but it's usually (though not always) the worst option. You may still get nasty things done to you.

7. Talk it through.

Share your ideas with an impartial and supportive person who:

- can listen to you, accept what you say, and keep it confidential;

- can help you talk it through and work out what you want to do.

Follow Your Bliss

There is something in you that knows when you are being true to yourself. There is something in you that knows when you are on the right track—or not. In your heart, you know with absolute certainty that it doesn't really matter what other people think or say—only you know what is best for you.

The sages remind us that there are many pathways to contentment, some ancient and others newly worn. But all of them demand you follow your heart—follow your bliss. In the widely broadcasted interview series *The Power of Myth* with Bill Moyers, Joseph Campbell said, "This is it. The end is the journey."

SECTION II

TAKING ACTION

18

PLAN THE PLAN

> Destiny is not a matter of chance, it is a matter of choice; it is not a thing to be waited for, but something to be achieved.
> —William Jennings Bryan

Before Marketing

Now that you have completed the groundwork, you are ready to sell yourself to the world. As California-based Debarah H. Wilson (http://amsquare.com/america/amerway/career.html), a nationally known career transition specialist, says, "A job search is nothing more than a marketing campaign and you are the product." Fortunately, you already know exactly what you have to sell—find it on your Skills Cluster List.

The Marketing Yourself section outlines all the details and strategies you need for maintaining your optimism and keeping on track. But before you rush to choose your letterhead, Howard Sambol, Assistant Director of the AOL Career Center, has some information that is sure to be of interest. As the by-product of guiding people through career transitions for over 15 years, Sambol has created a valuable catalogue of common career transition mistakes. His list of The Ten Most Avoidable Mistakes is part of Sambol's system called Career Crafting©.

Sambol (http://www.well.com/user/careerc/) suggests that awareness of these typical errors "will ensure you of not sabotaging yourself in the future. It will also ensure that you are working with the most current and advanced career development tools and support system available today." The Ten Most Avoidable Mistakes list is reprinted here with permission.

The Art of Successful Marketing: Prepare, Polish, Present

> The purpose of thinking is to collect information and to make the best possible use of it.
>
> —Edward De Bono

THE TEN MOST COMMON, AVOIDABLE MISTAKES DURING CAREER TRANSITION

☹ Avoidable Mistake #1

You combine your short-term financial needs with your long-term life/career goals and seek to satisfy both at the same time. You attempt to move forward without a secure financial base to build upon.

☹ Avoidable Mistake #2

You seek quick fixes or "Band-Aid" solutions. For example, you may jump from one idea to another trying to find "the answer." You fail to realize that finding a satisfying and rewarding job and career is a process that takes time, patience, and planning.

☹ Avoidable Mistake #3

You seek "success" as a picture in the outer world without having the essential clarity and self-knowledge needed for personal fulfillment.

☹ Avoidable Mistake #4

You attempt to progress without an effective support system for your career transition process.

☹ Avoidable Mistake #5

You follow the "shoulds" and "supposed-to's" of your parents or others rather than following your own truth. Or you try to reach conclusions about your future direction by using external authorities rather than discovering and following what you want for yourself.

☹ Avoidable Mistake #6

You believe that the only way you will be able to make money is by doing the same thing you've always done.

☹ Avoidable Mistake #7

You seek only advertised jobs and fail to use powerful networking strategies and entrepreneurial marketing methods.

☹ Avoidable Mistake #8

You blame yourself or others for why you aren't successful and dwell on past incidents or situations as the reasons why you can't move forward. As a result of this, you stay stuck in a victim mode rather than taking responsibility for your life.

☹ Avoidable Mistake #9

You do not take action because of lack of confidence and lack of clarity about what you want.

☹ Avoidable Mistake #10

You believe that once you've made up your mind about what you want to do, you can't change it.

What's Hot—What's Not

> Believe in yourself even when no one else does.
> —Harvey Mackay

Traditionally, your resume was your passport to a new job. Without a resume, it was highly unlikely that you would ever go anywhere interesting. But here, too, things have changed dramatically and with good reason.

For one thing, in recent years, resume services have become big business. Generally, for less than $100, a professional will take your background information and jazz it up so that you sound like the ideal candidate for the job you seek.

Of course, as recruiters and human resources departments received more and more of these high-powered documents, they became less and less impressed. Indeed, when it came to the interview, the interviewers often found that the person in the seat across the desk was not the person they had read about on paper. There developed an increasing sense that the resume does not tell the whole story—so much so that recruiters have begun to use resumes as a quick method for screening people out rather than selecting for inclusion.

A second point to remember is that because of the fewer number of jobs available, a resume is less useful for slotting yourself into that particular niche where you believe there is work that needs doing. Your background information may actually do you a disservice by appearing to pigeon-hole you or limit your capabilities.

In some cases, you may want to consider a resume alternative such as a "Creative or Marketing Package."

Marketing Yourself: Resume Alternatives

> The only way to differentiate yourself and gain lasting success is by creating raving fans.
> —Ken Blanchard

A Marketing Package

Since the impact of a resume is based solely on the reader's subjective opinion, it may be to your advantage to take another route entirely—rely on your own judgment for taking this approach. Since a Marketing Package cannot be judged on the same scale as a resume, it may compel the reader, at the very least, to think about you very differently from the rest of the applicants. In any case, high risk often delivers high rewards.

A young law student we know searched the tight job market with disappointing results. In a highly competitive marketplace, he found himself competing against "A" students and prize winners, to name only two of the obstacles he encountered.

Throwing caution to the wind, the young man created a glossy Marketing Package that appeared to be almost off-the-wall in terms of the norms and expectations of the big, traditional law firms. Many of the firms, quite naturally, did not respond at all. Several others, however, mightily impressed with the young man's creativity, risk-taking, innovation, and enthusiasm, called him for an interview. Bottom line, he did succeed in reeling in a super job with one of the most prestigious firms he had approached.

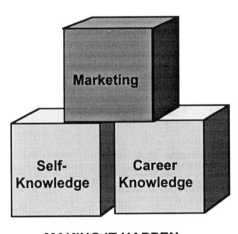

MAKING IT HAPPEN

A Marketing Package includes any of the information you think will pique the reader's interest. It may be presented in a twin pocket portfolio or even a gift box—depending on its suitability to your target audience—and it demands creativity in the assemblage and presentation of materials. It necessarily includes as much hard data as possible about your skills and what they prove but does not follow any preset format or formula.

A visually attractive Marketing Package demonstrates that you have carefully investigated the marketplace, that you have uncovered a niche for yourself, that you have something special to offer, that you are a valuable resource person in this particular field, and that you can solve problems.

A Portfolio

Simply put, your portfolio is a collection of your finest work and is, therefore, your best promotional material. Consider it your personal advertising campaign—with enough variety and flair to communicate your image and convey your message.

A portfolio is most often used for presenting creative work and, as with the Marketing Package or a good resume, compiling an effective portfolio is a time-consuming business. But if you need a portfolio, it is worth the hours you will invest.

With competition for work being what it is, you know that the number of individuals seeking work far outweighs the number of jobs available. If you are to be seen as a valuable asset to the organization, your portfolio must distinguish itself from all the others.

A portfolio includes carefully selected samples of the work you think promote your talents best. It should contain as many impressive samples as you need without appearing overloaded or disorganized; there is no preset format or formula.

A portfolio is usually contained in a zippered holder, but it may take the form of a video or slide presentation or any other format appropriate to the work you seek. It might include samples of your artwork, published articles by you or about you, a copy of a major report you wrote, and graphic charts of results you have achieved. Whatever you include, your portfolio demands creativity and visual appeal in the assemblage and presentation of materials.

Your portfolio demonstrates that you have carefully investigated the marketplace, that you are flexible and creative, that you have something unique to offer, that you are a valuable resource person in this particular field, and that you have a solid and uncommon ability to solve problems. Clearly, a portfolio that accomplishes these goals is not easy to assemble, but the good news is, it promises to be rich in practical pay-offs.

RESUMES

Writing a Dynamite Resume

A Traditional Resume

If you need a resume, it has got to work for you. Ideally, your resume is your advertisement—your personal billboard—with just enough space to communicate your image and convey your message in about 30 seconds. Its primary goal is to get you an interview.

Creating a good resume may take awhile, but it is worth the investment in time. Since recruiters are deluged with applications, you want your resume to stand out, to speak for you in your absence, and to distinguish itself from the rest of the pile, so you can get that coveted interview.

Do not assume that you can send the same well-written resume to everyone you plan to pursue. To get the attention you want it to receive, it must be patently clear that *this* resume is written specifically for *this* reader. If your resume looks like a form letter you created to cover all the bases, chances are you won't even get up to bat.

Keep your sentences short and use strong, vigorous verbs in brief, dynamic phrases; nouns should be descriptive key words. Be positive but never exaggerate to the point of dishonesty.

In summary, a well-written resume can get you an interview, so be sure that it:

☺ reads like a professional document

☺ includes strong action verbs

☺ contains descriptive nouns related to job duties or competencies

☺ is error free

☺ promotes your skills and abilities as benefits to the reader

☺ enhances your chances of securing an interview.

Paper

Use only standard $8^1/_2$ × 11-inch, good quality paper. Rag or recycled paper is ideal, but ordinary quality office paper is acceptable.

Color

White, ivory, or gray are good choices. The recycled "flecked" type of paper in a neutral buff or pale gray is currently in vogue.

Font or Typeface

Any font or typeface is acceptable as long as it is clear and easy to read. Detailed information on electronic resumes follows in the Electronic Resume Adaptations section.

Your aim in choosing your typeface is to find one that produces clear, sharp copies. Do not double space because doing so wastes advertising space and, believe it or not, it is actually harder to read.

If you have a computer, put your headings in boldface. You may even want to use two types of fonts or typefaces, one for headers and another for text. But remember, never use more than two, or your pages will appear sloppy and unprofessional.

Length

New graduates, students, or individuals with short work histories should be able to say everything on one page. For people with longer histories, an excellent resume is rarely more than two pages long, although this rule is no longer carved in stone. An on-line resume may be slightly lengthier because there are no page breaks.

Headings

Your headings may be centered or justified to the left. Your opening paragraph may be fully justified, but there is no need to fully justify the remaining text.

Headings should be highlighted so that they stand out for the reader. Information for each section may be indented to emphasize the content but remember to be consistent throughout.

Professionalism

Spellcheck, proofread, and proofread again. Tighten and polish your writing. Use high-impact verbs. Eliminate adjectives and "ing" words—they weaken your writing. Make sure all sentences are less than three lines long and all paragraphs are less than two-and-a-half inches long.

Printing

If you do not have a computer, have your resume transcribed onto a computer format and printed by a professional. Few home typewriters will produce the look you want.

The Resume Package

Your resume package consists of two components: the cover letter and the resume. Let's begin with your resume. Cover letter details begin on page 150.

Building Your Resume

> If I am not for myself, who will be for me?
> If I am for myself only, what am I?
> If not now...when?
>
> —Hillel

Format

There are essentially two types of resumes: chronological and functional (or a combination of the two). There are two media for sending either of these: paper and electronic. Whatever you choose, you will want to adapt the resume for the intended recipient and for the medium. (Here, we deal with paper resumes; electronic and scannable or Key Word resumes are covered separately under Electronic Resume Adaptations.)

The chronological format starts with your most recent history and proceeds backwards. It is the most common form for new grads and young people. If your work history is rather long, you may find this type of resume difficult, given your one- or two-page goal, but be selective.

Begin to assemble the sections by referring back to your Skills Cluster List.

Chronological Resume

In a chronological resume, work and education are placed in separate sections. Recruiters tell us they want only chronological resumes from recent grads or students, but use your own judgment on whether a chronological resume will do you justice. (Read more about chronological resumes on page 127.)

A chronological resume:

- works best for young people and recent graduates

- works well for job shifting within the same field

- is easy to manage.

Functional Resume

Functional resumes work best for individuals shifting direction or changing careers because they allow you to focus on applicable, transferable skills and talents. Based on your background, you must choose the format that works best for you. If your qualifications or educational history would appear weak in a chronological resume, use a functional resume. Or consider a combination of both.

A functional resume:

- emphasizes strengths and transferable skills

- de-emphasizes lack of applicable work experience

- de-emphasizes educational background.

Combination Resume

Once considered a "no-no," this format is becoming more common as the job market tightens.

Traditional Resume	
OUT	IN
text only	pretty layout, graphics, tables and visuals, appealing fonts
Courier®	bolds, italics, underlines and attractive fonts (no more than two)
several pages	one page goal, two pages for long work history, three pages maximum for executive levels
buzzwords, industry jargon, and acronyms	strong action verbs

Electronic Resume Adaptations

Just because everything is different doesn't mean that anything has changed.

—Irene Peter

On-line Resume

Given the new and extraordinary opportunities for making connections all over the world, the Internet provides a splendid medium for marketing yourself. But remember, a monitor or screen is a visual instrument. Should you decide to post your resume on the net, you will not be limited to one or two pages because the screen scrolls without page breaks. On screen, however, the visual appeal of your document is more important than ever.

For an on-line resume, use short bullet points and attractive visuals to draw the reader in. Learn to use Hypertext so that if a reader wants to delve more deeply, links to additional information are provided. With the popularity of World Wide Web browsers, a resume in HTML would not be inappropriate. One caveat—links to information outside of your resume can lose or confuse the reader.

To add flair and engage the reader, try simple but attractive graphics such as graphs, charts, shading, or interesting font selections.

The Key Word Resume

Ideas are useless unless used. The proof of their value is only in their implementation.

—Peters and Waterman

If you have already begun to mail out your resumes, you may have been startled to discover that the one you sent was unacceptable because it could not be scanned. With the high-tech revolution rolling nicely along, many companies currently in the business of hiring have instigated a high-tech process for matching job applicants with job openings. This computerized process is based on the "Key Word Resume."

In this system, your resume is scanned into the company's database. The computer then searches for key words that match the job description. These word matches are called "hits," and it may mean that the wonderful resume you wrote for a real live reader is totally ineffective for the electronic process. In fact, once scanned into the system, your resume may never be seen by a human again.

With a Key Word resume, visual appeal is secondary to its being scanned without corruption plus the need for "hits" when the computer does its search.

The astute job searcher will have both a traditional or readable resume and a Key Word resume available. In fact, it is wise to call the personnel department before you mail your resume and ask if resumes are scanned into the company's database.

Key Word Resume

OUT	IN
pretty layout	Helvetica®, Arial®, Swiss®, Courier®
bolds, italics, underlines, and interesting fonts	two, three, or even four (if you are at an executive level) pages is acceptable
one page goal	descriptive nouns, buzzwords, industry jargon and Key Words that describe job duties, experience, competencies, skills and abilities
strong action verbs	graphics, tables and visuals
text only	

Gonyea & Associates, Inc. is a Florida-based corporation specializing in the electronic (on-line) delivery of career, employment, and business development guidance and information. James C. Gonyea, the nationally recognized author of *The On-line Job Search Companion*, warns, "Key Word resumes are the integral ingredient of the job seeking process." Gonyea adds, "Key Words are the billboards that you can place on the Information Superhighway to draw the attention of employers to your employment availability." (Read more from Gonyea and his co-author, Wayne Gonyea, on the Internet at http://crm21.com/ or e-mail them at CareerPro1@aol.com.)

Gonyea says that, "Another way to look at Key Word phrases is to think in terms of job duties. The words and phrases that detail your job duties are the phrases—the Key Words—that provide your resumes with 'hits'." He further suggests that you observe the following guidelines in order to enhance the processing of Key Word resumes through the electronic system.

Key Word Resume Tips

- Left justify (do not fully justify) the entire document.

- Use a sans serif font in size 10–14.

- Avoid tabs.

- Avoid hard returns whenever possible.

- Avoid italic text, script, underlining, graphics, bold, and shading.

- Avoid horizontal and vertical lines.

- Avoid parentheses and brackets.

- Avoid compressed lines of print.

- Avoid faxed copies which become fuzzy.

In short, Key Word resumes must:

- be computer friendly

- use a regular, sans serif font such as Arial® or Helvetica® (no italics)

- use terms and acronyms for skills and experience that are relevant to the job you seek

- use nouns describing job duties such as Total Quality Management or TQM, Project Management, Operations, Strategic Planning, Communication Skills, or Sales Supervision

- promote your marketable attributes using the same Key Words and phrases the prospective employer or recruiter uses to search the database

- be printed on a laser printer or letter-quality inkjet.

The Writing Style

In compiling the sections for your compendium, keep the following guidelines in mind.

For paper or readable resumes, remember the importance of strong verbs and action-oriented language. Use words like improved, corrected, bettered, developed, produced, installed, enhanced, increased, augmented, expanded, succeeded, directed, managed, supervised, reduced, implemented, created, built, focused, clarified, generated, and enriched.

For Key Word or scannable resumes, pay attention to the buzzwords or phrases common within the industry, or words that describe job duties and competencies (refer to the Jane E. Doe sample resume on page 139).

If you are responding to an ad and are still in doubt about which are the Key Words to use, some of them can be found in the very ad you want to answer. For example, the following ads were taken directly out of a local newspaper; we have underlined the Key Words to make our point. (All trademarks are acknowledged to be the properties of their respective owners.)

GRAPHIC DESIGNER

Small Maritime company requires Graphic Designer with full knowledge of the Macintosh computer as well as the following programs: Illustrator, Photoshop, Freehand, & Quark. Knowledge of color separation & trapping for Flexo industry a necessity. Successful applicant must be highly motivated, results-oriented, creative, able to work flexible hours, work independently and possess strong customer relations skills.

ASSISTANT INTERNAL AUDIT MANAGER

This position requires a full and professional knowledge of accounting principles and practices and proficiency in generally accepted auditing standards. Requirements for the position include a C.A. designation together with a minimum of three years auditing experience in large not-for-profit organizations; working knowledge of EDP systems; above-average communication skills with a high degree of tact and diplomacy; the ability to plan, direct and control specific audit programs. Administration, operations, and management experience an asset.

The Elements

Your resume elements must be flexible so that whatever format you choose, the resume is effective. In building it, you would be wise to compile a compendium that allows you to pull out specific elements easily and to choose the appropriate "pieces" for the position you seek. If you work on a computer, create a selection of files under a resume directory. If you don't have a computer, a three-ring binder divided into accessible sections works just as well.

When it comes to pulling the pieces together for a prospective employer, the following items are fundamental:

1. Label each section clearly.

2. List work history/education in reverse chronological order.

3. Be brief but upbeat.

4. Be honest—employers do check.

5. Do not use friends or co-workers as references.

6. Match your skills and details to the specific job requirements.

The best resumes are comprised of the following elements, which you will use as section headings.

The Chronological Resume

1. Opening

   • Objective, career objective, or employment objective

   • Summary, profile, or experience

2. Skills or strengths

3. Work history or employment history (describing responsibilities and using two or three bullets to note accomplishments)

4. Education and continuing education

5. Professional affiliations

6. Community affiliations

7. Special interests

8. Special achievements or awards—if any

9. References (if you wish)

The Functional Resume

1. Opening

   • Objective, career or employment objective

   • Summary, profile, or experience (with skills or strengths)

2. Major accomplishments (broken into functional areas)

3. Work history

4. Education

5. Personal (professional and community affiliations, if impressive), citizenship, marital status (if you wish)

6. References (if you wish)

Select the appropriate combination for the job you seek from the above headings. If you decide to include a Reference section—and most resumes exclude it—it should simply read: available on request. That way, you are saving valuable space and creating an opportunity for the recruiter to speak to you directly. In addition, it allows you time to contact your references and remind them you are counting on their good word.

The Opening

The opening may consist of two parts: (1) objective and (2) summary. These are two separate and concise sections devised to catch the reader's attention and to give the reader a reason to read.

The opening introduces you to the employer in a few hard-hitting words that make a strong, positive impact. When the opening is solid, the reader reads on; if it is weak, your resume may be discarded immediately.

The best objective statement ties your talents directly to the job you seek. So, while you will have two or three or five of these openings stored in your compendium for easy access, you will change the words and details to fit the job opportunity. A good objective paragraph has three parts:

- title or function of the position you seek

- skills you bring to the position

- benefit of those skills to the reader's organization.

Here are some examples of good objective paragraphs.

Objective:

Position as Human Resources Manager using my proven talent as a superior trainer and course developer to take a leading role in the design and delivery of new corporate training initiatives.

Objective:

Position as a publications editor where I can apply my twelve years of experience as an academician, articles writer, and consultant to industry. A challenging environment that demands my superior writing and editing skills to prepare manuscripts for publication.

Career Objective:

Senior medical researcher in a stimulating, research-oriented pharmaceutical environment where I can apply my analytical and team-working abilities to the research and development of new products.

Here is an example of a good summary paragraph.

Summary:

A senior consultant with extensive experience in the design, marketing, and sales of innovative software products. Proficient in creative software design, my record includes successful projects in analysis, planning, and design and implementation of cutting-edge products.

Sample Chronological Resumes

JANE WHITLEY
15 Dalmatian Crescent
Naperville, IL 65376
(708) 555-9876

EMPLOYMENT OBJECTIVE:
Position as Human Resources Manager, where I can use my unique skill set to take a leading role in the design and roll-out of quality training initiatives.

WORK HISTORY:
May 1992–Present: Independent Human Resources Consultant

Consult to a broad variety of multi-national private and public sector organizations. Responsibilities include consulting on human resources needs; analysis of training needs; design and presentation of customized in-house skills seminars; design and delivery of train-the-trainer programs; implementation and roll-out of a multiplicity of OD initiatives.

Consulting and "hands-on" training experience include projects in customer service, managing change, team building, performance management, the learning organization, leadership, and coaching skills.

1987–1992 Manager, Training and Development, Superstar Packaging Company
* identified the skills required for success at Superstar Packaging
* improved the quality and delivery of skill development seminars by linking skills to business planning and Total Quality Improvement initiatives
* enhanced group dynamics by implementing annual strategic planning groups and establishing a standing committee for crisis intervention
* provided leadership to management; designed Superstar's first strategic HRD plan
* introduced over 200 different training programs to the company
* introduced professional skills and training strategies to managers across the United States

ACHIEVEMENTS:
* Designed and introduced a complete Human Resources Management System
* Successfully implemented a Quality Circle Program
* Launched a successful quarter-by-quarter growth profile
* Implemented field level forecasting system
* Instrumental in effecting $3 million in Federal support of training initiatives

EDUCATION:
Bachelor of Arts: University of Atlanta, 1982–1985
Ongoing skills development in HRD; the NTL Institute; University of Miami

SPECIAL SKILLS:
Published writer and experienced speaker; frequent presenter at international Human Resources conferences, including the American Society of Training and Development

BRIAN GREEN

612 Rue d'Ecole
75008 Paris, France
Phone: +33-1-5552-5657

EDUCATION

1994–Present PARIS SCHOOL OF MANAGEMENT, SORBONNE
UNIVERSITY
Joint Programme, International MBA/MIS (Graduation, March 1996)
• Vice-president, student council and editor, student newsletter
• GMAT 740 (99th percentile)

1989–1992 UNIVERSITY OF YORK LAW SCHOOL
Bachelor of Laws (Equivalent to American JD)
• *Attorney-at-Law for Ontario, Canada* (Called to the Bar in 1994)
• Canadian Department of Justice Scholarship
• Échange droit civil/common law, Université de Sherbrooke
• Early acceptance to law school on the basis of LSAT (99th
percentile) and GPA

1987–1989 UNIVERSITY OF TORONTO
• Ontario Scholarship

WORK EXPERIENCE

1994 GOVERNMENT OF MANITOBA—COMPANIES BRANCH
(WINNIPEG)
Project Consultant (Full-Time–3 months)
• designed and implemented a document processing system meeting legal and administrative requirements; cleared a 10-week
backlog in one month
• conducted an operational and legal review of administrative
functions

1992–1993 COLE, RAYE (TORONTO)
Articling Student (Full-Time–12 months)
• interned in the areas of litigation, real estate, and business law
• prepared for and conducted trials before courts and tribunals,
interviewed and prepared clients and witnesses, managed small
claims court actions, drafted legal documents and corporate analy-
ses, and researched to develop litigation strategies

1990–1991 GOVERNMENT OF BRITISH COLUMBIA—REAL PROPERTY
BRANCH
Policy Analyst (Permanent Part-Time & Summers–18 months)
• developed training seminars and information bulletins for a new
branch-wide information system
• mediated disputes between government officials and lawyers
• analyzed, interpreted, revised, and clarified government policy

1987–1990 BANKERS' TRUST (TORONTO)
Branch Supervisor (Permanent Part-Time & Summers–3 years)

- orchestrated the smooth operation of a branch of Canada's largest trust company
- managed a staff of 25 employees with daily transaction volume of $1–3 million

LANGUAGES   English, French

INTERESTS & PUBLICATIONS

- volunteer, Community Legal Aid and Ronald McDonald House (1990 & 1994)
- commentator, Fredricks Labour Law Reports, 1994 Series, Fredricks House, Toronto
- co-author, *A Student's Guide to Summer Positions*, 1994, Goforth Ltd., Toronto, 160 pages
- enjoy writing, sailing, skiing, travel, investing, music (old records & karaoke)

Sample Functional Resume

MARTIN BLACK
16 Northover Place
Palo Alto, CA 46734
415-555-3456

PROFILE

Hard working, highly productive, dedicated and motivated individual. Pursues success, initiates and achieves desired results. Over ten years as a self-starter focused on providing outstanding customer service.

SKILLS

- Outstanding interpersonal skills; proven ability to establish rapport and credibility quickly; consistent follow-through to build long-term, trusting relationships
- Accomplished in sales; excellent ability to close based on ten years of experience in a highly competitive marketplace
- Strong customer-service focus; solid ability to convey a service message by listening to customer objectives, meeting needs and tailoring solutions to marketplace conditions
- Highly productive; pursues challenge; approaches tasks with energy and a clear strategy comprised of precisely defined steps leading to results
- Superior listening skills to manage and negotiate objectives
- Open to new approaches to achieve desired results
- Manages time and work flow efficiently by identifying goals and accomplishing tasks quickly
- Collaborates and achieves cooperation and commitment of staff, resulting in a high quality of work
- Arranges financial strategy; quickly negotiates positive results under pressure

EDUCATION

B.A.—University of Chicago

REFERENCES

Available on request

Electronic Resumes

The Internet is a rich source of information for everyone, including job hunters and employers. Among the thousands of resumes on the net, Scott L. Hamilton, Steven Bird, and Gregory L. Gough have posted good examples of documents formatted for the screen. They are re-printed here with permission.

Please note that the underlined phrases are Hypertext which, when clicked on, link the reader to important additional information. Remember, too, that these resumes are intended to be read on screen, so the page breaks do not exist. To be fair, the reproductions on pages 134–138 do not do justice to the visual appeal of the on-screen design, but you can check out the originals on the Internet.

Scott L. Hamilton

Permanent Address:
235 Pinewood Ct.
Redlands, CA
92374
(909)792-7011

Current Address:
1008 Park St. Rm. 3
P.O. Box 05-85
Grinnell, IA 50112
(515)269-3228

Electronic Address:
hamilton@math.grin.edu
http://www.math.grin.edu/~hamilton (personal home page)

This document is Netscape Enhanced.
Also available: Non-Netscape, PostScript, and plain text.

Summary

Looking for entry-level (or possibly higher) employment in the computer industry. Willing to relocate. Four years of Internet experience with extensive knowledge of a variety of areas (see below) and capable of learning virtually any system, application or software.

Skills

Operating Systems:	Languages:	Applications/Standards:
☐ Unix (esp. HPUX and Linux)	☐ C and C++	☐ HP VUE Windowing Environment
☐ VMS	☐ Pascal	☐ X11 Windowing Environment
☐ MS-DOS	☐ HTML	☐ Common Gateway Interface (CGI)
☐ MS Windows	☐ Scheme	☐ Internet mail protocols
☐ Macintosh OS	☐ Perl	☐ World Wide Web/ Netscape
	☐ TeX	☐ Gopher
		☐ GnuEmacs

Employment

May 1994 - Present: Information System Maintainance, Grinnell College Computer Services
Part- and full-time adminstration and maintainance of internet informations systems based on Gopher and World Wide Web.
Duties included:
☐ the installation of software on a VAX VMS system
☐ the modification, maintainance and support of local information systems, including the creation of support programs in C and Perl
☐ the coordination of several information sources and an assitant
☐ authoring Gopher and World Wide Web documents and programs

Education

Three years at Grinnell College, Grinnell, IA
☐ Majors: Computer Science, Religious Studies (currently on leave)

General:

☐ Excellent communication skills (Former member of National Forensics League)
☐ Notable Computer Aptitude
☐ Four years of Internet experience
☐ Learns New Systems/Applications Quickly

References:

John David Stone, PhD
Lecturer in Computer Science and Philosophy, Manager of MathLAN, Grinnell College Dept. of Math and CS
Kirt A. Dankmyer
Academic Computing Specialist, Carswell Hall, Wake Forest University
Deb Roepke
User Services Specialist, Grinnell College Computer Services
Brian McMahon
Academic Programmer, Grinnell College Computer Services

Steven Bird

41-S Quail Hollow Rd.
Greensboro,NC 27410
(910) 294-2547
e-mail:SteveABird@aol.com

❑ **Career Objective:** Entry into the field graphic design and/or web page design

❑ **Skills Summary:**

- ❑ Experience with Photoshop 3.0, Illustrator 5.5, and QuarkXPress
- ❑ Knowledge of **html**
- ❑ Strong sense of design
- ❑ Quality draftsmanship with or without a computer
- ❑ Other applications: Word Perfect 3.0 and Transparency 1.0 for Macintosh

❑ **Accomplishments:**

- ❑ Created the illustrations and promotional flyers for the book *Everything I Needed to Know About Money I Learned in Arithmetic Class*
- ❑ Produced the interior art for the CD *Once Around the Lake My Dear* by the band Touk
- ❑ Currently building a website for Touk
- ❑ Designed posters for theater productions and band appearances at Guilford College. Click here or here to see them.
- ❑ Drew an adventure comic strip for submission to King Feature Syndicate. To take a look, click here.
- ❑ Drafted a T-shirt logo for the band Stuck Mojo

❑ **Related Experience:**

- ❑ Assisted Buzz Setzer in coloring *Hawkman* and *Damage* for DC Comics
- ❑ Worked as an intern at WORDWERKS, a graphic design company in Atlanta
- ❑ Selected for an intensive workshop in graphic design at Georgia Southern College

❑ **Education:**

- ❑ University of North Carolina at Greensboro, Greensboro, NC 27412-5001
  - ❑ Graphic Design with a Computer Fall 1995-present
- ❑ Guilford College, Greensboro, NC 27410
  - ❑ BA with honors in History
  - ❑ 3.4 GPA
  - ❑ Four-year full tuition Honors Scholarship
  - ❑ Thomas Thompson History Scholarship Sophomore year
  - ❑ Algie I. Newlin History Scholarship Junior year
  - ❑ Physics minor
  - ❑ Study abroad semester in Italy, Spring 1992
- ❑ International Baccalaureate Diploma from North Fulton High School, Atlanta, GA 30305
  - ❑ Soviet exchange program
  - ❑ Mexican Exchange program

Thanks for coming by. You're guest number
199
since 2/23/96. Hope to see you again soon.

Please click here to browse my electronic portfolio.

Please click the button to e-mail me.

Back to my homepage.

GREGORY L. GOUGH

72223.3216@compuserve.com
Click here to download resume (MS Word)

CAREER OBJECTIVE

To obtain a position in a computer systems consulting firm, or in an information systems department of a well-established company, that provides an opportunity for education, advancement, and stimulating challenges for highly motivated, intelligent, and creative people.

SKILLS AND STRENGTHS

Technical

Hardware: IBM PCs, PC compatibles, Macintosh, Networks, IBM mainframes, SUN SparcServer, HP and other scanning/imaging hardware.

Operating Systems: Windows 95, Windows NT, Windows 3.1, Windows for Workgroups, OS/2, DOS, UNIX, Macintosh.

Network Systems: Novell, Microsoft Networking (NT, Windows for Workgroups), IBM LAN Server, Microsoft LAN Manager, Internet, TCP/IP.

Development Tools/Languages: Visual Basic, PowerBuilder, FoxPro for Windows, KnowledgeWare ADW, DESIGN/1, FOUNDATION, Paradox Application Language, C, COBOL, Pascal, BASIC, Assembler, HTML.

Other Software: Lotus Notes, Word, Excel, PowerPoint, Access, Paradox, dBASE, Lotus 1-2-3, WordPerfect, various scanning/imaging software, Rumba, Extra! for Windows, various Internet browsers and authoring tools.

Personal

Skilled young professional with integrity. Committed to quality and excellence. Challenged by difficult technical assignments. Analytical and innovative in problem solving. Intelligent and flexible in interpersonal relations. Dedicated to personal and organizational development in a competitive environment.

EDUCATION AND TRAINING

Education

Bachelor of Science in Computer Information Systems and Accounting, David Lipscomb University, Nashville, TN. May, 1991.

Technical Training (Andersen Consulting)

- Computer Application Programming School (3 weeks)
- Systems Design and Systems Installation Schools (1 week each)
- Client/Server Applications School (3 days)
- Information Engineering Concepts Training (3 days)
- PowerBuilder Development Tool Training (1 week)
- FoxPro Application Development Training (1 week)
- OS/2 2.0 and IBM LAN Server Training (1 week)
- KnowledgeWare Advanced Development Workbench Training (3 weeks)
- New Age Systems Workshops (1 week total)

RELEVANT EXPERIENCE

**July 1991 - Senior Consultant, Andersen Consulting, Technology Organization,
Present   U.S. South Region**

Prince George's County Courts, Upper Marlboro, MD (JusticeLINK Electronic Filing and Imaging System)

- Served as technical analyst and support for development of an electronic filing system using imaging and Lotus Notes on wide-area network.

State of Tennessee, Department of Human Services, Nashville TN (Tennessee Child Support Clerk System - TCSCS)

- Served as lead technical analyst and supervisor for development of a FoxPro for Windows child support system implemented across 20 clerk sites.
- Designed, implemented, and assisted with managing development of a multi-user Clerk System for child support payment processing, case maintenance, and interfacing with the Tennessee state mainframe child support system.
- Determined equipment requirements and configurations for multiple clerk sites, including workstation requirements, server sizing, network configurations, remote access, and mainframe communications.
- Developed and supervised implementation of project development standards.

State of Tennessee, Department of Human Services, Nashville TN (Tennessee Child Support Enforcement System - TCSES)

- Served as lead analyst for development of a PC-based forms processing sub-system for TCSES.
- Designed and implemented architecture for IMS mainframe-to-PC forms messaging, on-line forms requesting, and form template management.
- Designed and developed a PC Forms application utilizing Visual Basic, DDE, and Microsoft Word to print forms in local IV-D and clerk offices.

Large Entertainment/Resort Company, Orlando, FL

- Served as lead technical architect and analyst for development of a customer information and reservation system.
- Assisted with setup and configuration of client/server development environment using Windows, Novell, PowerBuilder, and Sybase SQL Server.
- Developed PowerBuilder pilot application and graphical user interface front-end for AS/400 and Unisys mainframe reservation applications. Utilized DDE to communicate between PowerBuilder and emulation sessions.
- Created system architecture deliverable documenting user types and locations, application architecture, and network configuration.
- Established project standards and procedures for version management, data recovery, and application design.

Large Hotel/Casino Corporation, Memphis, TN

- Established and served as administrator for development environment using LAN Manager, Windows for Workgroups, and DESIGN/1.
- Performed detailed evaluation and selection of development tools and operations management tools.
- Supervised client personnel in creation of project workplans and budgets.

Large Overnight Package Delivery Corporation, Memphis, TN

- Developed an IBM LAN Server network environment for a KnowledgeWare Application Development Workbench (ADW) pilot project. Managed roll-out to production environment supporting over 70 developers.
- Served as LAN administrator for LAN Server and Novell 3.11 client/server development environments.
- Created and supported repository management procedures for consolidating project and corporate data models.
- Conducted user training sessions on data model consolidation.

Other Experience - Business Systems Consultant and Contractor

Vanderbilt University School of Medicine, Nashville, TN

- Designed, developed, and trained users on an Ob/Gyn resident physician experience tracking system using Visual Basic and Paradox.
- Provided reports to national Residency Review Committee for certification of Ob/Gyn resident program.
- Assisted with design of new record-keeping, data entry, and reporting procedures for resident physician experience.

NJC, Inc., Consulting Engineers, Nashville, TN

- Developed fire emergency mechanical systems sizing software for use in mechanical engineering design specification.
- Created automated fee calculation and estimating system for partners of firm.

Ted Wynne & Associates, Inc., Consulting Engineers, Nashville, TN

☐ Created automated electrical panelboard design system with interfaces to AutoCAD for electrical engineering department.

FishWagon of Harrisburg, AR

☐ Assisted in the development of a customer information database and truck routing system for eastern United States fish delivery business.

HONORS AND ACTIVITIES

☐ Peak Performer Award - Andersen Consulting
☐ David Lipscomb University Half-Tuition Honor Scholarship
☐ Dean's List; Alpha Chi National Academic Honor Society
☐ Intramural Volleyball and Tennis Teams (1990-91)
☐ Dormitory Resident Assistant (1988-90)
☐ Chorale and Acappella Singers (1986-90); Vice President (1987-88)
☐ Singarama (1987-90); Musician-Guitar, Keyboard, and Bass

REFERENCES AVAILABLE UPON REQUEST

Click here to go to my Home Page!

More on Key Word Resumes

In an article worth reading on the Internet at http://crm21.com/, Wayne M. Gonyea of Gonyea & Associates, Inc. writes:

The standard resume, no matter how effectively designed, executed or presented, is no longer adequate to meet the demands of electronic/computer scanning. Computer scanning is necessitating a significant re-engineering of the concept and process of using resumes in job hunting endeavors.

Gonyea adds that according to OnLine Solutions, Inc., a company charged with the primary responsibility of uploading full text resumes into the Information Superhighway, "Although resumes can be received by OnLine Solutions electronically via e-mail and diskette, fully 85% of them are received on paper, thus requiring scanning."

Traditional vs. Key Word Resumes

Debarah Wilson, a Career Transition Specialist in Menlo Park, California, was originally a resume writer specializing in Key Word resumes, that is, resumes designed to be scanned by a computer. Wilson states, "The average job seeker or career planner has not been fully informed about the extent of computer scanning of their resumes or the pronounced need for properly prepared Key Word resumes." Further, from teaching classes in Key Word Resume Preparation, Wilson found that, "The Key Word resumes can be best understood by observation." So, Wilson has prepared the following sample Key Word Resume, which is reprinted here with permission.

Sample Key Word Resume

JANE E. DOE—MANAGEMENT GENERALIST

1234 Elm Street
Anywhere, USA 95959
101-456-1234

ADMINISTRATIVE MANAGER, OPERATIONS MANAGER, DIRECTOR OF ADMINISTRATION, CHIEF OPERATING OFFICER, RETAIL MANAGER, PUBLIC ADMINISTRATION DEPARTMENT HEAD, GENERAL MANAGER, MANAGEMENT CONSULTANT

Summary:

Results-oriented professional with administration, operations, and management experience in start-up, reorganization, or expansion in small to mid-sized companies.

Supervising: operations; accounting; accounts receivable; accounts payable; payroll; budgeting and forecasting; cost accounting; collections; facilities management; employee development; marketing and product positioning; advertising; merchandising; inventory control; public relations; customer support; new business development; strategic planning; materials management; administration.

Excellent interpersonal skills, team player and ability to work well with all levels of an organization. Effective presentations, verbal and written communication skills. Well-developed organizational, project management, trouble-shooting and problem-solving abilities.

Computer literate. Proficient in WordPerfect 5.1, 6.0, Word for Windows, Lotus 123, and PC File. Working knowledge of Microsoft Works, Excel, Quattro Pro, MAC programs and DOS.

BBA, University of Anywhere, Management, Accounting and Human Resources, 1973.

Career History:

1991–present: BRANCH ADMINISTRATOR, Acme Widget Manufacturer, Somewhere, IL., Largest widget manufacturer with revenues of more than $32 million, over 350 employees and seven branches in Illinois.

Supervised 46 employees in administration; accounts receivable/payable; sales support; human resources; employee development; quality control; customer service. Directed the daily operations of the branch and increased profitability. Developed a self-directed management team to implement progressive changes. In 1993 moved to 1st place in customer service, profitability, overall performance, and realized a 44% growth.

In collections decreased the days outstanding for delinquent accounts. The days outstanding dropped from 49 days to 36 days in 3 months, and the branch was no. 1 in collections in 1992.

Wrote a Sales Coordinator Training Manual, after evaluating all of the procedures required for tracking new business from sales to installation. The manual was adopted company-wide.

Implemented a customer-driven program that follows TQM standards and has reduced the number of customer complaints and increased customer satisfaction.

1988–1991:   MANAGEMENT CONSULTANT, Jane Doe Consulting - New York area; Dallas, TX; and Portland, OR. Provided consulting to companies that were in start-up situations, reorganization or that needed computer and new business development assistance.

As COO, managed a potentially $2 million company and developed the client tracking process for a start-up career marketing company. Had the business operational in six weeks.

Reorganized an executive suites company in Dallas, TX, as CENTER MANAGER. Rehired and trained 16 employees, developed the budget, and increased revenues by 45% in the first 5 months of 1990.

Expanded a major party linen company in Queens, as GENERAL MANAGER. Set up the northern Virginia distribution facility. Hired and trained all personnel, developed the budget and all accounting systems, set up all office procedures and delivery schedules which allowed for the center to be up and running in 20 days, and attained revenues within 2% of goal.

Created Courthouse Square Association in History, OR, as volunteer DIRECTOR in 1988.

Developed goals, directed public relations and fund raising for the square, thereby increasing the public knowledge of the availability of the facility for private functions. Worked with the City Council, Redevelopment Agency, private investors, and venture capitalists.

1983–1987:   OWNER, GENERAL MANAGER in New York City, of two specialty retail toy stores, and three department stores specializing in seasonal and Christmas items.

Directed advertising; public relations; accounting and tax compliance; merchandising; inventory control; sales supervision; budgeting and forecasting. Supervised 100 employees.

1977-1983: DIRECTOR, Police Administrative Services Bureau, Any Police Department, Middle City, NY.

Supervised 146 employees; the day-to-day operations; Accounting Division; Property Management; Evidence Management; Building Services Division; $30 million budget; Human Resources.

Additional Training:

Re-engineering the Corporation-1994; Conflict Management-1994; Training the Trainer-1993; Self-Directed Team management by Blanchard-1993; Managing Negativity in the Workplace-1993; Total Quality Management, TQM, courses-1993; Criminal Justice System and Civil Service-management courses from 1977 until 1983.

Writing a Winning Resume

When it comes to resumes, Wendy Enelow (http://amsquare.com/ america/advantag/winning.html) is a well-respected pro. The on-line author of *Writing a Winning Resume* (major sections are excerpted below with permission), Enelow agrees with other experts in the field. Says Enelow, "Resume writing is marketing. It's that simple!

To create a powerful and successful resume that will advance your search campaign, you need to identify the features and benefits you have to sell to a prospective employer. Then carefully, and with great thought, provide that information in a resume.

Let's suppose I've run an advertisement for a CEO, MIS Director, National Director of Sales & Marketing, or Manufacturing Plant Manager. And now, only one week later, I have 429 resumes on my desk and at least 100 phone messages from interested applicants. It would be easier to just do the job myself (if I knew how!) than to try to work my way through this task.

So, I spend the next week sifting through resumes that all say the same thing. Programmers tell me they write code, systems analysts tell me they design new systems and applications, chemical engineers write that they develop processes for chemical manufacture, and CIOs tell me that they direct the corporate information management organizations.

I KNOW THESE THINGS! That's what the job is.

Looking at what I think is resume #388, something is different! This resume says something. It highlights projects, achievements, special task forces, and a host of other interesting and distinctive activities. I want to meet this applicant!

Now, is that applicant you? It certainly can be if you learn the tricks and techniques to effectively market yourself through your resume."

Enelow Strategy: The Sales & Marketing Game (reprinted with permission)

The resume is a great tool. There are really no rules, no definitive procedures that dictate how you prepare your resume. The choice is yours. The opportunity is there to sell your achievements creatively and aggressively to effectively position yourself above the competing applicants and get in the door for an interview. Just remember, the purpose of your resume is to get the interview. Resumes don't get jobs.

Yes, of course, you need to include the "typical" resume information—professional work experience, educational background, teaching experience, technical qualifications, and professional affiliations. Equally important is the emphasis you place on selling your career successes—special projects, new systems development, productivity improvements, quality improvements, reductions in operating expenses, and more. The list goes on and on. A few examples include:

- Directed the development and implementation of a new corporate Information Management System to replace obsolete technology. Managed project from initial conceptualization and systems specification through the entire programming, configuration planning, installation, and technical training cycle.

- Redesigned internal product scheduling procedures and reduced net days per project by 32.

- Redesigned engineering processes and expedited daily production by 18%.

- Identified cost overrides in contracting data processing fees, renegotiated vendor agreements, and saved over $2.3 million annually.

By including this type of specific information, you are "teasing" the prospective employer. It is important that you provide detailed information to substantiate not only your qualifications, but also your ability to contribute to the corporation and effectuate positive change. In today's economy, everyone is suffering—from the large corporate giants of yesterday to the small, high-tech companies. Money is tight, competition is fierce and economics are forcing massive change.

Companies need expertise and the ability to produce. Your job is to use your resume as an effective sales tool that will demonstrate your knowledge, achievements, and capabilities. As your prospective employer, "tell" me not only what you have done, tell me how well. Be careful, however, about "overkill." Achievements must also be within the realm of reality (and documentable)! Prepare a resume that will sell your talents, technical qualifications, career history, and achievements.

Visual Presentation: The "Make It Look Good" Game

Yes, visual presentation matters. In order to sell yourself as a professional, you must "look" like a professional. With the advent of word processing, desktop publishing, and laser printers, there is no excuse for a nonprofessional presentation.

The one-versus-two-page dilemma is a constant point of concern. Years ago, the "Resume God" said, "Let your resume be one page." And it was law. But times have changed, the competition is fierce, and you must make every attempt to aggressively "sell" your qualifications. If two pages is required, so be it. You will find that the response to your job search campaign will be directly dependent upon how well you've marketed your qualifications and achievements, not on number of pages.

The Painful Truth

Another international expert, Steven Provenzano, reports, "Too many job hunters downplay their resume as just a piece of paper that usually doesn't work. Maybe you're one of those who believes, 'My resume isn't perfect, but I'll explain myself in the interview,'" says

Provenzano, who writes extensively on-line (http://amsquare.com/america/ advanced.html). As the author of *TOP SECRET Resumes & Cover Letters* (Dearborn Publishing), Provenzano's suggestions are invaluable. Provenzano continues:

> But here's the catch: You may not get the interview for no other reason than your resume, which often gives employers their very first impression of your professional standards and talents. Yet even top-flight executives can have trouble writing a decent resume. They're not sure how to make the link between what they really want to DO in their next job with the needs of potential employers.

> An effective job hunt in the 90s means having a complete, professional job search strategy, and your resume must be a key part of that strategy.

Key Factors in Resumes

Provenzano's article on Key Factors is reprinted here with permission.

KEY FACTORS

Here are a few Key Factors and philosophies developed and used with great success over the years. These Key Factors help explain why most (possibly yours) resumes fail, and how you can really stand above the crowd and get noticed. When you implement these ideas in the next update of your resume, you will almost certainly have better success in getting more interviews.

Key Factor #1: What Employers Really Want to Know—"What Can You Do for Me?"

Look at the hiring process from the employer's point of view. There you are with a stack of resumes on your desk and a job to fill, right now. You've got some key requirements that candidates must meet before you'll even consider calling them in for an interview. All you want to know from each person "sitting" on your desk is:

> **What can you do for me?**
>
> **How can you fill this job effectively?**
>
> **Why should I talk to you?**

So you start reading resumes, and you see the same old stuff employers have been getting for decades: page after page of job descriptions (i.e., Chronological resumes).

Wait a minute. As an employer, I want to see what you can do for me, but all you're telling me is what you've done for someone else. Of course this is important, and I need to scan your previous work experience and accomplishments. But does all this really apply to my situation? Of course not, and I really don't have time to read 10 or 20 years of your work history before I decide to call you in.

This is why purely Chronological resumes, for the most part, are on the way out, and why the next Key Factor is so important.

Key Factor #2: Your Resume Must MARKET YOUR ABILITIES.

Take a moment and really think about what this means. Does your current resume really market your most applicable skills and abilities, or is it a listing of your past? You must extract your most applicable skills and abilities from your past work experience and sell them at the very top of your resume in a summary section, titled "Profile" or "Experience." Your Summary gives you control over your resume and lets you focus on key points.

As for Objectives, they can be very useful when targeted and concise, but leave the section out if you're afraid it may block you from consideration for certain positions. In that case, give the reader a focus with the first points of your summary. If you do use an Objective, recruiters say it shouldn't be "rosy" and "must quickly define what the applicant is looking for in one or two sentences."

It's important to note that unlike a Functional resume, the Summary section in a Combination resume is not really about previous jobs, but rather highlights those skills and abilities you believe are most important and relevant to the position you're seeking right now, whether acquired through work or school.

This is the heart of a Combination resume format. It combines a modified Functional (ability/achievement) resume with a Chronological (job listing) resume. This gives you a two-pronged approach and the best of both worlds. Your job descriptions substantiate your abilities on top.

If this sounds easy, it is. But it only works if you use clear, concise language describing tangible, no-nonsense skills:

"Skilled in payroll processing, audits, and inventory control...

"Effectively hire, train, and supervise staff in...

"Plan and implement strategies for capital investment; assist in mergers, acquisitions, and financial planning...

"Proficient in COBOL, C++, AS 400, and Lotus...

"Experience in long- and short-term strategic planning..." And so on.

Always steer clear of using fluff words in your summary such as "Self-motivated, hands-on professional with an excellent track record of...." Let's face it. The first two items in this sentence could be said about almost anyone. As for your track record, let the employer decide if it's excellent by reading about your abilities (on top) and your duties and accomplishments (under the Employment section).

Avoid the ubiquitous (and space-filling) "References available upon request" at the bottom of your resume. If employers really want your references, they'll ask.

When conducting a confidential job search, consider "CONFIDENTIAL RESUME" at the top of your resume and/or stating this in your cover letter. Always respect the reader's intelligence!

That having been said, take a look at this:

Key Factor #3: Do the Thinking for the Employer.

Employers don't really want to think when they're scanning resumes. Why trust an employer to study your entire work history and hope they find something interesting? Most resumes get only a few short seconds to grab the reader's attention. How is that possible when some of your most applicable skills are buried (or only implied) under a job description, perhaps one near the bottom of the page? Never expect your resume to be read all the way through.

Do the thinking for the employer and tell them exactly what you think they want to hear (assuming it's true) right on top in your summary section.

If you have a Chronological resume, no matter how well it's written, it's still a listing of your past, and, therefore, not job-specific or future-oriented. Your resume must be a brief advertisement, not a history of your past. How many resumes are actually written along these lines? Very few.

By the way, Provenzano is a Certified Professional Resume Writer and offers a free resume analysis if you phone him at 1-800-322-8621 or e-mail ADVRESUMES@aol.com.

20

WHIPPING THE WILLIES:
MORE SPECIFICS FOR MARKETING YOURSELF

The way to get good ideas is to get lots of ideas and throw the bad ones away.

—Linus Pauling

If even contemplating the path ahead gives you the willies, you can reduce your anxiety considerably by knowing you've covered all the details. So, here they are.

The Letterhead

The letterhead you use is an important part of the image you wish to convey. If you have a good laser printer and a simple graphics software package, you can easily create your own letterhead. If you choose to go the professional route—usually the best decision—almost any good print shop can produce exactly what you need at a very reasonable price.

Choose a clean, professional-looking letterhead from the printer's sample selections. Avoid fancy fonts, bright colors, and unusual layout or design.

The Business Card

Like your letterhead and resume, your business card is a vehicle for marketing yourself in print. It demonstrates your style and professionalism, so, by all means, consult with a printer or typesetter.

Your business cards should match your letterhead in color, style and typeface. They should project a clean, professional image and include your name, address, and phone number. If you have a fax or e-mail address, include those, too.

All the Letters You'll Ever Need

> Look within and seek THAT.
> —Jalaluddin

Cover Letters

Because a positive or negative response to the written word is established within the first two lines of correspondence, you must target the reader immediately. Open with a reader-centered statement and make it clear that you understand the reader's needs and can meet them. At the top, indicate your understanding by identifying what the reader wants to hear or by mentioning the position for which you are applying.

Always write *to a name.* We have all received a "Dear Householder" letter and consigned it to the rubbish pile unopened. We trash it because we know that any letter meant for everyone is not meant for us. "Dear Sir/Madam" has a similar effect. It tells the reader that you do not know, nor do you care, who the reader is. "Dear Sirs" or "Gentlemen" is equally unsuitable in today's business environment. As a job applicant, you must indicate, in every way, that this letter is of specific interest to this particular reader.

Use positive language and a sincere tone. Lead with your ace. Good news at the top sets up a positive reader response.

Write in a comfortable, personal style, but do not confuse personal with casual; you want to build a bridge, not a barrier, between writer and reader. Establish rapport by eliminating jargon and writing to the reader in human, everyday language.

Use the shortest possible word to convey your message accurately. Don't say "utilize'" when you could say "'use." Don't write "facilitate" when "help" will do the job. Do not send the reader to the dictionary; this is not a homework lesson. Don't chatter on with irrelevancies that confuse the issue; this is not a leisure activity for the reader. Business clichés and plastic formality depersonalize your message, and, happily, they are no longer considered good form.

Today's cover letter is clear, concise, fact-based, and action-oriented. Above all, it is reader-centered and demonstrates, within the very first paragraph, that you have identified the reader's needs and can meet them.

To further indicate that your letter and resume are one of a kind, do a little research; try to include a piece of the company information you gathered. Go to the library and pick out the words the company has used to describe itself; use those words to describe yourself. Talk to people who know the company and get some industry-specific or "inside" information. Then, in your cover letter, you can mention one or two problems that your qualifications address.

If the company has advertised a position, select Key Words from the ad and use those precise words in your letter. For example, if the ad calls for a team player with strong leadership abilities, describe yourself that way.

Be sure that your cover letter:

1. indicates that you know something about the reader's operation

2. states why you want to work specifically for the company to which you are writing

3. reads as though this company is the only one receiving your resume.

Worth Noting

A letter to the business editor in a city newspaper was written by a man who had recently advertised an available position. Stunned by the sloppy responses he received, he wrote to the paper:

I recently placed an ad in your paper for a position in my company and received 632 responses. Right now, there are probably 623 people who think they were perfect for the job but believe they were eliminated for a variety of inconsequential reasons. Not true. They were eliminated because their responses indicated they were not worth calling for an interview.

An alarming number of resumes included nothing to indicate that the applicant was responding to a specific ad for a particular position; I gather these folks expected me to read through pages of information and try to figure out how they might fit my needs. Many respondents faxed resumes without a fax cover or cover letter, expecting me to guess why I might be interested in them. Many did use a fax cover, but it was either cute or silly—in either case, unprofessional. A huge number of respondents wrote "To Whom It May Concern" when the ad specifically asked for a response to the Sales and Marketing Manager. (Only two people bothered to phone and ask for my name, and they both got interviews.)

A startling number of responses included major grammatical errors and misused words. The spelling mistakes were particularly shocking because those errors could have been eliminated by a simple spell check.

So, if you didn't get a call back, don't blame me. You did it to yourself.

Cover Letter Outline

Date

Name
Title
Company Name
Address

Dear _____:

Begin with a sentence telling the reader why you have chosen to write to this employer or where you heard about the job opening. Give the reader a reason to read in one sentence; link your background or skills to the position you seek.

Briefly describe your interest in the position or industry. Tie your background or specific qualifications to the position or industry. Mention a special achievement or skill that could be seen as a benefit to the employer.

Ask the reader to read your resume. Emphasize pertinent data.

Close with a statement indicating an earnest interest in an interview and a request for a meeting. Say when you will call back for a confirmation of your meeting.

Sincerely,

Signature

Typed Full Name
Enclosure: Resume

Sample Cover Letters

<u>BRIAN GREEN</u>

612 Rue d'Ecole
75008 Paris, France
Phone: +33-1-5552-5657

Ms. Maxine Turner
College Relations
Apple Computer
1 Infinite Loop
Cupertino CA USA 95014-2084

Dear Ms. Turner:

As a joint International MBA/MIS student at the Paris School of Management, I am looking for a challenging position in the technology industry.

Solid experience in both the public and private sectors has given me a broad perspective and problem-solving track record to bring to Apple. Working for Canada's largest trust company, I observed the impact of technology and operations on customer service and revenues. As the company's youngest branch supervisor, I used my creative problem-solving skills and made specific recommendations to senior management. These recommendations were accepted and resulted in measurably improved customer satisfaction and employee productivity.

I was involved in a variety of projects for the Canadian government, from creating a training system for private lawyers to developing the communication strategy for the implementation of a new, revolutionary land ownership information system. Building on my past experience, my studies now focus on using technology for strategic advantage in an increasingly global and dynamic marketplace.

I offer Apple and its clients:

- outstanding interpersonal skills and creativity
- an international perspective
- proven analytical, negotiation, and team skills
- a strong and diverse education in law, management, and technology.

I look forward to discussing the opportunities for a mutually rewarding relationship and will call you in two weeks to explore the possibilities. In the interim, please contact me if you would like any further information.

Sincerely,

Brian Green

Brian Green
Resume enclosed

July 15, 1996

Ms. Netta Star
Human Resources Manager
Stellar Communications Inc.
145 Starlight Blvd.
Burlington, MA 01889

Dear Ms. Star:

I read with interest your ad for a layout artist at Stellar Communications Inc. and wish to apply for the position.

Currently, I am a freelance layout artist designing print ads for a number of high-tech companies. As a creative, hard-working graphic specialist, I have a solid reputation as a talented artist with an ability to take a concept straight from the drawing board right through implementation and delivery. My interpersonal and team-working skills are superior; my "hands-on" experience with Apples and Macs is particularly applicable to the position I seek.

With eight years in the field of graphic design, I have developed an expertise in the design and delivery of high impact print ads. My early training as assistant editor of *Fancy Photography Magazine* brings additional leadership skills to the job; my involvement in designing the *Inform Our Youth* brochures, plus my background as an illustrator of children's books, create a unique constellation of specialized skills that dovetail precisely with your needs at this time.

I will be pleased to meet with you at your convenience and provide any additional information you may need. I will call you in two weeks to set up an appointment, or, if you prefer, you can reach me directly at (415) 555-7766 or write to me at the address above.

Sincerely,

Jaime Rogers

Jaime Rogers

Enclosure: Resume

January 16, 1997

Mr. Mark Watterstein
Personnel Manager
Kalamari Industries
78 Browning Road
Naperville, IL 60567

Dear Mr. Watterstein:

In response to your advertisement in the *Naperville Sun*, January 15, 1996, I wish to apply for the position described as a Visual Merchandiser Display Builder.

With six years experience in the field and a demonstrable record for creative talent and design expertise, I am a graduate of the Glendon School of Applied Arts with a double major in visual merchandising and display building. I excel in a team-based environment under production time and cost constraints, and my leadership and interpersonal skills are the added value I offer Kalamari Industries.

I am available for an interview at your convenience and would very much like the opportunity to discuss my qualifications for the position in more detail. I have enclosed my resume and will call you in two weeks to set up an appointment. If there is any additional information you need, please call me directly at (708) 555-1212.

Sincerely,

Max Farger

Max Farger
Enclosure: Resume

The Thank You Note

Every meeting or interview you attend should be followed immediately by a pleasant note of thanks written on your letterhead to the person with whom you met. Should that person be creating a short list from the long list of all interviewed applicants, your note may be precisely the evidence needed to include you on the short list.

Post-Interview Thank You Note Outline

Date

Name
Title
Company Name
Address

Dear _____:

Begin with a sentence expressing thanks for the interview.

Mention a company need and how your background and skills meet that need. Identify a specific issue that was stated by the interviewer and use it to sell the benefits of hiring you.

Close with a statement indicating an earnest interest in working with the company and a reminder of how you can be reached.

Sincerely,

Signature

Typed Full Name

Sample Post-Interview Thank You Note

STEVEN SMITH
          1226 Broadway • New York NY • USA 10023 • +1-(212)-555-0995

December 7, 1996

Mr. Igresh Venugopal
Schollard Consulting Associates
698 East 64th Street
New York NY 10022

Dear Mr. Venugopal:

Thank you for taking the time to interview me yesterday. I found our discussion to be stimulating and enjoyable.

I hope you will agree that the focus at SCA is well-suited to my background. Being able to use a diverse set of skills to solve unique and difficult problems is what attracted me to consulting and to SCA, in particular. I would welcome the challenge of working with your colleagues to provide first-rate service to your clients and the opportunity, as you highlighted, to collaborate on creating unique and targeted solutions to concrete business problems.

Thank you again for your time and interest. I am most eager to work for Schollard Consulting and hope to hear from you soon. Please call me at 555-0995 if you have any other questions about my candidacy.

Sincerely,

Steven Smith

Steven Smith

JOB HUNTING FOR RECENT GRADUATES[1]

If you want to be happy for an hour, take a nap.
If you want to be happy for a day, go fishing.
If you want to be happy for a week, kill and eat your pig.
If you want to be happy for a month, get married.
If you want to be happy for a year, inherit a fortune.
If you want to be happy for life, love your work.
—Confucius

In the 90s, a law degree is no longer a guarantee that you will have a career in law. Similarly, sixteen years spent at home raising a family does not consign you to the kitchen or nursery for eternity. In an increasingly competitive marketplace for skills and ideas, students entering the workforce, just like individuals carving a new career path, must have the information necessary to compete for a declining number of job opportunities. With this need for knowledge in mind, the following section has been created for your use. It will take you step-by-step through the job hunting process, beginning with the decision to search for work and ending at the time a job offer is made.

Knowing Yourself

The key to any successful job search is knowing yourself and being able to articulate your interests and ambitions, and your strengths and goals, both in person and on paper. Because any job search is of a personal nature, this section of *Your Outplacement Handbook* is, as always, user-specific; spaces have been left for you to fill in personal information, deadlines, and checklists to ensure that you have not missed anything. You will want to check back to the work you did in earlier sections to transfer all the salient information as needed.

Being Yourself

There is no doubt that the "hunt" process is stressful. The material you send out must be flawless, and your social skills must be the best they have ever been. While it is true that the decisions you make and the image you present will help to determine the career path you take, it is important to remember that being yourself throughout the process increases the odds that your future job is a fulfilling one.

So, by knowing the process, by knowing yourself, and by being yourself, you will have the best chance of finding a rewarding position without the need for transcendental meditation. Try to have a good time. And good luck.

Steps to Getting an Interview

> Great minds have purposes. Others have wishes.
> —Washington Irving

1. Write the ideal resume and cover letter and mail them to your prospect.

2. If, after two weeks, you have received no response, phone for an interview appointment. Write down the time and place.

3. Two or three days before the scheduled meeting, phone to confirm the date and time.

4. Attend the interview appropriately dressed and prepared to answer questions and sell benefits.

5. Follow up the interview with a thank you note.

6. After every interview, record your experiences and keep them in your file for future reference.

Keeping Records

Beginnings are always messy.
—John Galsworthy

Looking for work is a job and should be handled with the same attention to detail as any job you undertake. Keeping an accurate record of your progress and findings is important. Set aside a section in your notebook for records or use a system of index cards.

Sample Interview Record

Interviewed by:

Date:

Company:

Address:

Phone:

Position:

Referral source:

Original communication: date of contact (cold call, letter, resume)

Thank you: (date sent)

Referrals/suggestions from the interview:

Interview lessons:

Problem areas:

Strategies for improvement:

Follow-up plan:

The Interview Process

It is no easy task to send out all those resumes or to center mailing labels perfectly on 20, 50, or 100 envelopes. Then there is the terror of follow-up calling and the possibility that you were right after all, that your dog is really the only living thing that needs you. But, after making the call, or calls, you now know that there is a future out there. You have not crumbled into dust from rejection, and perhaps you even have an interview. This part of the job search is considered by many to be the most difficult and stressful step.

Now, more than ever, a positive attitude will help you to survive. Just remember that almost all job hunters eventually secure work and that where you work now is not necessarily where you will work for the rest of your life.

Accessing Your Resources

We detail this in the next section—using your network, checking the ads, researching possibilities, the information interview, and so on. When you have a reasonable list of possibilities, you send your resumes to them. If you are looking for the kind of work that merely requires you to fill out a job application, some of the following may not apply.

Dialing for Dollars

Before you phone your prospects, remember that you will be dealing with three kinds of people. The first kind are people who are responsive. They are the people who received your resume and wrote back to say that they will be in touch or that you should call them to arrange an interview. The second kind are the people who reject you. They will be people who have written to say that although you have wonderful qualifications and although you are an outstanding person and upstanding citizen, they will not be calling you. The last kind consists of individuals who have not responded to you at all.

If you are expecting a call, sit beside your telephone on the appointed day. If need be, cancel your dentist and hair appointments. Be back from Europe. Make sure that every other living creature that could possibly touch or breathe on your telephone is aware that the telephone is your telephone. No prospective employer wants to play telephone tag with you, so do your best to be "it" when the tagger phones. At the very least, use an answering machine with a recorded message that sounds business-like.

Practice Makes Perfect

No matter how many interviews you may have been offered, you will be required to handle stress and organize your time, all the while sending out those warm-fuzzy feelings that say to the people doing the hiring that you are Mr. or Ms. Right. The best way to accomplish this with ease is to be practiced in the art of being interviewed, and the best practice for interviews is interviews. But if you haven't had any interviews lately, there's no sense worrying about it now. Rather, try to schedule your first interview early on Monday morning with the organization or company in which you are least interested. If you do this, you will have an opportunity to practice your interview skills under the least possible stress; if you blow it, it won't make a major difference because you didn't want the job anyway.

Another idea is to hold a mock interview with a friend, partner, relative, or teacher using the questions in this chapter as a guide. Yes, you may feel incredibly foolish, but the next best thing is really the very best thing if you have no other recent interview experience.

Let's say you were participating in a 500 km bike race next spring. If you practiced all winter on your stationary bike, you still wouldn't be familiar with the course; you may not even know how to handle bumps and turns. But at least you would have the strength and endurance to go the distance. You get the picture.

Organizing Your Interviews

Design a table or calendar to help you schedule your interviews. In many organizations, the recruiting process goes on all the time, and it is unlikely that the time of day for your interview will affect your chances of being hired. So, if you are not a morning person, schedule afternoon interviews.

If you are lucky enough to have several interviews, allow two hours between them. That's one-and-a-half hours at one place and another half hour to find the building, the elevator bank, the bathroom, and the reception desk of the next. You really will need this extra time. If you are in a big city, avoid the underground tunnels as much as possible; they are navigable only by veterans of the system, and it is simply too easy to get lost. If you find during an interview that you are running late, politely inform your interviewer that you must leave for another appointment but would it be all right if you dropped by later to meet some other members of the company (if you want to).

Confirmations

You may or may not receive a written confirmation of your interview. If you do not, be sure to confirm it yourself by phone two or three days after receiving the interview request. Call once again, a day or two before the interview, to reconfirm and to obtain the name or names of the interviewers and, perhaps, the intended length of the interview.

In *The Firm*, the protagonist researched the careers of all the people who were to interview him (you can too); the interviewers were very impressed that the applicant made that special effort to learn about their law schools and areas of interest. Of course, they eventually tried to kill him, but that rarely happens in real life.

Getting Around for the Physically Challenged

Most downtowns are not readily wheelchair accessible. Buildings that are accessible often have ramps in obscure places; only someone familiar with the buildings could find them. People who have trouble getting about should try to find these ramps and elevators beforehand and should try to allow extra time between appointments. Public transportation is usually not accessible, and special services are notoriously unreliable for things like multiple appointments. You may, therefore, have to rely on cabs.

Different Types of Interviews

The Initial Interview

For this, the most common format, you can expect to meet with one or two interviewers. The atmosphere of the interview is a relatively relaxed, respectful, and friendly one. The goal of this interview is for a company to acquaint itself with the applicant, to judge the applicant's interpersonal skills, and to elicit important information. Depending on the level and type of job for which you are applying, if the interviewers are impressed with you, one of the types of interviews that follow will often occur.

Serial Interview

If your initial interview went well, it may be followed by introductions to others in the company. The introductions may be on a formal basis, by having you join the new interviewers in another meeting room, or on an informal one, by giving you a tour of the offices and casually introducing you to others. The key to this interview is to be alert and to answer every question as if it were being asked for the first time.

Pay attention to what each new person says. Try to gauge which individuals like you. If you really hit it off with someone, you may want to return to gain more information and to lobby. Remember, the bigger the company, the greater the pull of people in high places; it would not hurt to have Ms. Head of the Accounts Department go to bat for you.

The "Wine and Dine" Interview

Applicants whom the company wishes to impress are often taken out to lunch. This lunch may follow the first interview, or it may be a prelude to a second interview. The group at lunch will usually consist of the individual who conducted the first interview and a senior manager who may be on the hiring committee, either of whom is working in a field in which you have indicated interest. The conversation in this case is likely to be very casual, but under no circumstances should you drop your guard.

Every move will be watched and, as spelling errors can ruin a resume, bad manners may make the most eloquent lunch guest look like a know-nothing. If you feel your table manners are lacking, pick up one of the many books available on the subject. The guru has long been Amy Vanderbilt, but there are other good ones, among them Miss Manners herself. If you find yourself completely stuck about which fork to use or whether to eat the pickle with your fingers or your fork (use your fingers), look to others for clues. This is no time to be eating lobster, which is impossible to eat gracefully, or even pasta, which has a nasty habit of splattering sauce on you at the most inopportune times. Grilled or roasted chicken or meat is the best bet. Here are some common etiquette crimes; the list is by no means exhaustive:

Crimes Against the State of Etiquette

The Knight in Tarnished Armor

Remember men, if you wouldn't do it for a man, don't do it for a woman. Don't be pulling chairs out for the women— they may consider you sexist. With doors and elevators, the soft rule is that the person in front opens the door or gets on first, but do whatever is comfortable. Your interviewers will often make room for you to pass first, in which case you should—seniors often allow others to go before them. There is no explanation for this, but it is true that heads of state usually have the motorcade or entourage clear the path.

The Hockey Player

Never use your knife to push food around your plate. If you can't get a morsel with your fork, leave it. It is permissible to use a piece of bread as a "pusher," but this trick is hard to master and should probably be avoided. You should also never scrape food off your knife and onto your fork.

The Toddler

Don't talk while you're chewing. You knew this.

The Fencer

Avoid wielding your knife and fork to emphasize what you are saying.

The Godfather

Do not tuck your napkin into your collar. It goes on your lap while you're eating, on your chair while you're in the bathroom or at the buffet, and on the table when you're finished.

The Dentist

Don't pick food out of your teeth during or after the meal. Go to the bathroom if you need to do this.

The Supermodel

Do not apply makeup at the table.

The Vulture

You may be allowed to do it with family or friends, but here you may not eat what others leave on their plates.

Above all, try to remain calm; answer questions politely and to the best of your ability, and be prepared for any situation. You are permitted exactly one alcoholic drink and that is if, and only if, everyone else is having one. It should last through the meal. Smoking is not mentioned here because you can't—no matter what.

Other Interview Formats

Group Interview

This type of interview often requires you to meet with a recruiting team or committee. One of the problems with this style of interview is knowing to whom you should address your answers. Begin the answer by speaking to the person who asked the question; then make eye contact with the other interviewers to include them in the conversation as well.

Stress Interview

In this, the most difficult type of interview, your patience and stress management are tested with several techniques. These methods include: keeping you waiting before the interview commences; staring at you without interruption; interrupting frequently; asking rude, personal, and often irrelevant questions; and leaving the room or looking preoccupied.

The best way to handle this stressful situation is to recognize it and to remain calm and polite. Getting upset or arguing with the interviewer will not help the interview. This is a test, and the best response is to take it in stride and to show the interviewer that you are mature in your handling of the situation. But if this is the company's style, you may not want to work there anyway.

Government Interviews

Most government departments are relieved from the "get to know you" interview and, instead, must employ a standard, formal procedure. The interviewers are provided with a set of questions that must be asked, and they are required to write down your responses. Do not be alarmed; they are not doing this just for you. And try to be patient while they do all that writing.

Information Interview

This type of interview, sometimes called the Investigative Interview, can be wonderfully helpful in your job search. It is an interview you arrange so that you can gather information about the company or industry with which you are meeting. You may want to talk to someone who is doing the job you want to do, so that you can get useful inside information. (More about this in the Marketing section.)

In this kind of interview, your goal is to present yourself as a person who is investigating opportunities in an area in which you can make a contribution. In theory, you are there only to learn more about the challenges and to gather the inside dope. In reality, you usually have a hidden agenda—to present yourself as someone the company needs. That is, secretly, you hope to send this message: I want to impress you as a person who is worthy of future consideration. Notwithstanding this goal, you should never ask for a job in this situation.

Since most everyone these days is aware of the hidden agenda in these Information Interviews, it is becoming harder and harder to arrange them. With downsizing fever raging across the continent, you may be perceived as a threat by the very person you have asked to help you. Perhaps that person worries that his or her job will disappear tomorrow, or that you seek his or her soon-to-be-vacated slot. Given these concerns, you may find it easier to arrange an Information Interview out of town where you will not be seen as a threat and where you may actually get information you can use to help you identify a niche for yourself.

If leaving town is not a reasonable alternative, be certain that your prospect knows you are simply researching the field—that you are not, at this time, looking for work. And should a job offer follow the interview, be wise enough to say you must consider the offer for a week or two, or you may be perceived as deceptive.

Remember the rule: DO NOT ASK FOR A JOB! But since you have asked for this meeting to gather information, by all means be prepared to take notes. And, of course, leave your business card. If you are asked for a resume, offer to send one immediately.

Informational Interview Steps

1. Write or phone for the informational interview. We find that a simple letter outlining your reason for a meeting, followed by a polite phone call to set the appointment, usually results in success.

Informational Interview Request Outline

Date

Name
Title
Company Name
Address

Dear:

Begin with a sentence explaining why you are contacting this particular reader; mention a referring person if one exists.

Briefly describe your background and your interest in the industry. Specifically state that this is a request for information, not a job, and that you need only about twenty minutes of the person's time.

Close with a statement explaining that you will phone to set up a convenient appointment.

Sincerely,

Signature

Typed Full Name

Sample Informational Interview Request Letter

April 8, 1997

John Lassinger

Manager, Product Development
ReRoute Household Products
97 State Street
Atlanta, GA 30319

Dear Mr. Lassinger:

Leo Fields suggested I contact you to learn more about ReRoute Household Products and the recycling industry.

After working in advertising and promotions for the last eight years, I am currently considering a career change. While I am certainly not ready to make the switch, I do want to learn more about your industry and the opportunities that exist within it. If you would allow me twenty minutes of your time to help me gather some information and to hear your suggestions, I would be most appreciative.

I'll call you next week to see if we can set up a convenient time for you.

Sincerely,

Fred Foster

Fred Foster

> If you prefer, you may make a cold call, but be prepared to open with something like:
>
> > "Hello Ms. Martin. My name is Jackson Adams, and I am considering a career change. I'm very interested in the XYZ industry, but I need to learn more about it. Michael Jones suggested I set up an informational interview with you."
> >
> > Or, "I read about you in the newspaper," or "your name was suggested to me by your colleagues."

2. Two or three days before the scheduled meeting, phone to confirm the date and time.

3. Arrive early enough to check yourself in the washroom and to appear prompt.

4. Attend the interview. Begin with thanks for the meeting and take a few minutes to establish rapport. Remember, this is an informal interview, and the person with whom you are meeting is doing you a courtesy; they should not feel they are being interrogated. When you are both comfortable and relaxed, move on to your prepared questions such as:

   • Tell me what you do.

   • What attracted you to this field?

   • What skills are required to work in this area?

   • What are the opportunities for advancement?

   • What is the general starting salary? (This is important information to have when you are actually offered a job.)

   • What do you suggest I focus on if I want to work in this field?

   • Do you have any other advice for me?

   • Who else do you suggest I talk to?

5. Leave at the agreed upon time—or at least make the offer. Most often, you will be invited to stay a little longer, and you may do so, with thanks. But do not overstep the bounds of good sense.

6. Follow up the meeting with a thank you note.

7. Record your meeting.

Post-Informational Interview Thank You Outline

Date

Name
Title
Company Name
Address

Dear:

Open with a statement of thanks. Comment on the reader's helpfulness.

If possible, comment on a remark the interviewer made that was particularly helpful to you. Briefly mention your next step and how the interviewer assisted you in moving forward in your information-gathering process.

Close with another brief statement of thanks and a promise to keep the reader informed of your progress.

Sincerely,

Signature

Typed Full Name

Sample Post-Informational Interview Thank You Note

May 7, 1997

John Lassinger
Manager, Product Development
ReRoute Household Products
97 State Street
Atlanta, GA 30319

Dear Mr. Lassinger:

Sincere thanks for meeting with me yesterday to discuss the opportunities and challenges at ReRoute Household Products and within the recycling industry. Your insights and advice were certainly helpful. I left the meeting feeling that I now understand the needs of the industry and that I have the skills to meet them.

Since our meeting, I have arranged to meet with Marsha Genoa at ReRoute and Lance Brittin at General Recycling. And, as you suggested, I will focus on developing my proficiency in creative problem solving.
OR
Thank you also for referring me to Marsha Genoa at ReRoute and for your suggestion that I explore creative problem-solving techniques. I will keep you updated as my search progresses.

Sincerely,

Fred Foster

Fred Foster

Telephone Techniques

He that will not apply new remedies must expect new evils.
—Francis Bacon

In your job search process, the telephone is a tool you need to use well. E-Span is one of the oldest career services operating on the Internet and World Wide Web (http://www.espan.com/docs/telefon.html). Committed to continually expanding its resources to serve individual consumers and human resource professionals, E-Span offers the following telephone tips, reprinted here with permission.

Telephone Tips

Using the telephone well will make your job search more effective, reduce your stress, and actually shorten your job search. The telephone is a tool. Using it to its fullest capacity—without overusing it—takes practice.

1. **Plan your calls.**

   Determine the purpose of your call(s). Are you following up on a resume and letter sent to an employer? Are you trying to schedule a networking meeting? Are you following up after an interview?

2. **Set an objective for each call.**

   Depending upon the purpose of the call, your objective shifts. Aim for a brief exchange of information. If the resume was received, ask about the current stage of the selection process. Have interviews already been scheduled? If you are following up on a letter requesting a brief networking meeting, your goal is to schedule a brief meeting convenient to the other person. If you are following up on a positive interview, your objective might be to express continued interest and to inquire about the expected schedule for second interviews.

3. **Script your calls.**

Before making each call, jot down a list of Key Words to remind yourself of key points. Then, actually write out the main parts of your conversation. These parts should include:

- greeting the person by name and stating your name

- briefly building rapport and stating the purpose of your call

- inquiring whether the other person has a few minutes to talk with you

- listening to their answers and proceeding accordingly

- if your timing is not good, inquiring as to a better time to call back—and then calling back at the agreed time

- if your timing is good, succinctly asking one to three questions

- thanking the person for their time and mutually agreeing to a next step.

4. **Rehearse your calls.**

Adults learn by doing, not by thinking about a behavior. Calls for job search purposes are different than calls either for purely business or social purposes. Practice so that the words flow easily for you.

5. **Present an upbeat, confident image on the telephone.**

One trick is to put a mirror in front of you so that you sit up straight, smile at yourself, and thereby send your positive body language to the listener through your voice. Try it! It works!

6. **Minimize telephone tag.**

Ask about the best times to return calls (often before 8 A.M. or after 5 P.M.). If the person you are calling is currently "on another line" or "just stepped down the hall for a minute," wait on the line for a few minutes.

7. **Buy and use an answering machine or voice mail service.**

Record a professional message. Your "cute" five-year-old—on tape or actually answering the telephone—does not send a professional message to business callers. (After your job search, you can have any message on your tape.) For now, your answering machine is an example of your credibility to a potential employer.

8. **Train your family to take messages well.**

Your future employment may depend on your responsiveness to a message left to arrange an interview or follow-up interview. Have paper and pencil by all telephones so that you or your family can easily take a message or write down directions and appointment times.

9. **Return calls promptly and professionally.**

Carry notes with you if necessary so that you can return calls retrieved when you are not at home.

10. **Pace your calls.**

Leave no more than one message a day. If you have left your name and telephone number three times with no returned calls, ease up for a week. Ask the receptionist (if there is one) about the best times to call. Put this person on your weekly call list for three weeks. If you have left three messages a week apart (following the initial three messages), take this person off of your list.

11. **Expect to make three calls before connecting with the other party.**

Even in the 80s, the likelihood of connecting on the first call was only 17%; the likelihood of connecting on the second call was 23%. Practice your patience. These are the 90s, and everyone is even busier! Even you are not available to take every call when it comes in the first time.

Prepare to Dare

> The only joy in the world is to begin.
> —Cesare Pavese

What You Wear Says How You Fare

Dress conservatively. While the outfit you wear will not get you the job, it may, unfortunately, exclude you from getting it.

Both men and women should wear suits when applying for indoor work. However, you should also be comfortable as you will often have long days if you are in the graduate recruitment process. Whatever you do, do not buy new shoes the day before your interviews; the discomfort and blistered feet will not be positive additions to your day. If you should have any questions as to the style of a specific company, contact them. But beware—just because people in government don't always wear suits does not mean you should not wear one to the interview.

The key is to be neat and well-groomed without being flashy. The safest attire is a navy or gray suit with a white shirt or blouse and black shoes. Women must wear hose, even if it's ninety-five degrees outside, and a low heel is preferred to flats or spikes. Anything else may make you look overconfident, daring, or quirky. Do not wear your Disney tie or peace necklace. Nor should you wear the one-ounce gold nugget ring your uncle brought you from Las Vegas. It is also customary to bring a briefcase and a note pad if you are applying for a professional position and plan to take notes.

It would be naive to think that there is no discrimination in some organizations, and what you wear will sometimes make you a target.

One student with excellent credentials was practically hired by the interviewer, only to be shown the door when a senior partner saw his long hair, a custom of the applicant's people. The partner explained there was no "fit." If you feel there has been discrimination in your interview, you may wish to report the incident to the proper authorities. Unfortunately, the discrimination is usually so subtle that you would not notice it unless you had worked at the organization for some time.

Attending the Cocktail Party

In many professional firms, recruiting is done before graduation and in bunches, so there may be another challenge ahead of you. Imagine this: You're nearing the end of your interview. Things are going well. You have discussed your sterling academic record, your valuable years of community service, and your travel experiences in Asia. Then, just as you are leaving, someone mentions to you that there will be a cocktail party at 6:00 and that it would be nice if you could make it.

Cocktail parties have three objectives. First, the company wants to find out how you behave in a "social" situation. Even though you won't be invited to another event for ten years—when you make partner—the cocktail party will determine whether or not you have the right stuff to work at that particular company or firm. The second purpose is to expose you to as many senior employees as possible. Maybe it was just a fluke that the interviewer liked you; perhaps one of the managers knows your family and can tell the others about the time you were sent to the office in elementary school for jumping out the window during math class. Finally, the cocktail party is a chance for the firm to gather information. They want to know with whom else you interviewed, how did it go, and what do you think so far. The firm has asked you on a date. Whether an engagement will follow depends on your performance that evening.

Deciding to Go or Forgo

If you absolutely hated the company, don't go. It will be a waste of your time and energy, and the free food is not worth the boring conversation. You could be trapped by a senior manager and quizzed on your knowledge of marketing theory. Take the evening off and prepare for other interviews.

On the other hand, if you are curious and would indeed like to meet the members of your potential employer's group, you should attend. Standing up the company does not get you in their good books, and they do keep track of who shows up and for how long. If you have been invited to two or more parties on the same night, go first to the one at the company you liked most, then try your best to make the others. You should stay at each for at least an hour, so some time management is in order. It is perfectly acceptable to excuse yourself after that time to attend another party. If, however, things are going really well—and they're only going really well if someone on the hiring committee tells you that they are—you may extend your stay at any one of the receptions. Just remember that a no-show may mean a no-go with the other firm that has invited you.

Appearance

At the cocktail party, you should look as incredible as you looked at 9:00 that morning, and you should be dressed for business, not partying. Interviews rarely go beyond 5:00 P.M. Take that hour before the party to find a washroom and clean yourself up. Since many companies recruit in the warmer days of spring, you may look a mess.

Every hunter should have discretely hidden on his or her person a comb and toothbrush (or at least breath spray). Of course, you put on three ounces of unscented deodorant in the morning, so body odor won't be a problem. If by some fluke you are in the least bit sweaty, find the coolest air conditioning vent you can and dry out.

So, now you are in the washroom. Wash your face and hands. Check everywhere for tears in your clothing, mustard on the cuff, or gum on the shoes. Brush your teeth and hair. Women should touch-up makeup if they're wearing it. The wisest of all will have stashed a fresh shirt or blouse and a complete selection of hair sprays, gels, and powders in a locker or nearby friend's house or place of work. A shower, if at all possible, will freshen you up; just make sure you have enough time so that you don't arrive with wet hair. Sparkle. But please, no perfumes or colognes. Nobody wants to be reminded of Obsession commercials every time you walk by.

Arriving

If you show up at the time you are told, you will most likely be the only one there. Be fifteen to thirty minutes late. No later than that, because you have work to do and will need the time. The reception desk may have name cards laid out. Put yours on and walk into the reception room relaxed and ready to smile.

Someone, usually a member of the hiring committee, will greet you at the door. After a brief "how's it going" and some small talk, you will be steered towards someone else and dropped off there. Good-bye to the person you sort of knew. Hello, stranger. Now you must make pleasant conversation with someone you've never met before. And you'll be doing it all evening.

If you are not met at the door, pause briefly and then get yourself a drink. The only thing you should pick up is a glass of white wine. Any of the hard stuff, and you'll look like a lush. Cola or ginger ale, and you're a dull teetotaler. White wine is standard and won't stain too badly if you spill it. You are not going to drink it anyway, so don't worry if you don't like it. Persons on the AA program are exempted from this procedure, as long as they don't choose this as the time to discuss the twelve steps on the road to recovery. With your drink, which you will hold in your left hand (so that you can shake hands with your right), you may now proceed.

Your Immediate Job

Your objective at this event is to make a favorable impression on as many members of the firm as possible. Don't waste your time speaking with other students, even if they are friends. Find a company representative who is alone, shake his or her hand, and introduce yourself. You will not be intruding—they are there to meet you. If you soon discover that your conversation partner is another student or the caterer, make a polite excuse and get out fast. Remember, you have a very short time in which to work. When speaking with one person, maintain eye contact. Be conscious of nervous habits such as touching your face or constantly sipping from the glass of white wine in your left hand.

If no one is alone, it is quite acceptable to introduce yourself to a group. Pick out an interesting one and approach. If you are feeling a bit shy, join another student who is already engaged in conversation on the pretense of being interested in how things are going. Try not to hover around; find an opening (polite people will make one) and enter the circle. When there is a pause in the conversation, make eye contact with the person on your right and introduce yourself to each person in a counterclockwise direction. If the person on your right avoids eye contact, start in the other direction. As you introduce yourself to a person, make that all-important eye contact and smile as you shake hands.

About the handshake—it should be a firm, one-pump. Practice on someone if you think you need to. No bone-crushers, limp wristers, double-handers, or hangers-on. Just shake and drop. Men who shake women's hands as if they are greeting the Queen look like anachronistic jerks and will not score points; a male-female shake should be the same as that between two men or two women. The only time a man may hold a woman's hand upright in his is when he is auditioning for a role in *Gone With the Wind*. Nobody told you to wear a Civil War costume, did they?

Now, you are now speaking with one or more persons. Eye contact, eye contact. Concentrate on what people are saying. Don't sip. Be an active listener by smiling at witty comments (or attempts to make them) and nodding occasionally. Be casual. Pretend you're having fun. Of course it is unlikely that you are having fun because you are under stress; after all, this is work.

What do you talk about with all these strangers? Remember, you are out to show them that you are the type of person they want, need, and will enjoy at the company. They do want to hear about your trek in Nepal, your work with the local hospital, your favorite subject in school (actually, nobody cares at all about this but you should jump at any opportunity to prove you know at least something about something— just keep it short), what you did during the summer and what other jobs you have had and enjoyed. They do not want to hear about the D you got in Civ Pro, how you were arrested last week at the border, about your parents' ugly divorce, or about your activities with the local chapter of the Communist Party. It's small talk—the soft sell.

Steer clear of issues like religion and serious politics, human rights, and money. If you have any questions on the company's attitude towards a "sensitive" topic, try to meet later in the week with one of the seniors, preferably one you met at the party and liked. On second thought, it's better not to ask. If the firm is progressive, they will probably want to tell you about it. If it is not, they will lie and say that it is. Try to get your information from an outside source. Be observant; if everyone around looks a certain way, its probably no accident.

You will be pressured to disclose your feelings about the company and about others at which you have interviewed. This pressure exists despite protests to the contrary and is quite annoying. If this is the company for you, by all means say so—companies don't want to waste their time on individuals who are not interested in them. If it is not, use your best judgment in what you say. This may be difficult because you have to be guarded, frank, discrete, and open at the same time. You have to keep them interested, because it's much too early to burn bridges, yet you must be truthful. Definitely do not lie; that sort of thing will come back to haunt you.

Conversations will last about fifteen to thirty minutes. After that, someone will make an excuse and go to the bar or the washroom or over to meet someone who has just arrived. They are probably not coming back. This behavior should be expected. While it would normally be considered rude, in this situation it is vital that you meet as many people as possible.

As soon as you are left alone, find someone else to talk to. Fill your dance card—now is not the time to play wallflower. This is probably the most difficult type of socializing you'll ever have to do, so don't feel incompetent if you are stressed-out. Unfortunately, you have no choice —the recruiters will vote on you, and you must get as many as possible on your side.

On Eating and Drinking and Thinking

Even though there will be an abundance of food and drink at most cocktail parties, do not plan to enjoy either. Remember that hour you took to get ready? Well, in addition to transforming yourself into the perfect new employee, you also grabbed a Big Mac so you wouldn't be hungry later on. There are simply far too many risks involved when one eats at a party. Too many opportunities to spill and slobber, too much likelihood of getting something stuck in your front teeth. You can't talk with food in your mouth. You can't shake hands if you have a glass of white wine in your left hand and an egg roll in your right. If you are offered food, a polite no-thank-you will suffice.

If you absolutely must eat—and you couldn't possibly because you ate before you came—play it safe. Stick to carrot sticks, mushrooms, and anything else that can't break up or open and fall onto the floor or, worse, onto you. Avoid dips and sauces. Crackers are deathtraps. The only way they don't break is if you put them completely into your mouth at once. Do that, and you multiply by ten the chance that someone will hit you on the back forcing you to spray cracker dust everywhere.

Should you decide to play daredevil and go for something like a cheese puff, the procedure is as follows: take a napkin in your right hand and place it under the glass of white wine in your left; eat the puff; take the napkin with your right hand, wiping your fingers, and dab one corner around your mouth; ditch the napkin at the next opportunity—even if you plan to eat again in thirty seconds—on the food table, in a waste basket, or discretely in your pocket. Not worth the effort, is it? And if someone asks you a question in mid-chew, you lose.

As for drinking, you don't. Get drunk, and you will have lost any chance you had to get the job. Save the drinking until after you're hired. Even if you can tolerate a lot of alcohol, you don't want to be seen floating over the bar; you certainly don't want to smell like you're tanked. Your glass of white wine should last at least an hour. Period.

Smoking

No matter how many people are smoking at the cocktail party, you will not. Smoking has become socially unacceptable and is now seen as a sign of a weak character. Smokers should carry extra breath mints, sprays, and even a pocket-bottle of mouthwash; try nicotine gum if you like but make sure you are never seen chewing it or any other type of gum. If you must smoke, do it outdoors where no one will see you. Washing your hands and brushing your teeth will help get rid of the smell but will not eliminate it completely. The best course of all is to quit a week before the interviews, but this route may prove unbearably stressful for real smokers. After you're hired, you may smoke as much as you want, outside, of course.

Though smoking may be the great sin of the 90s, nonsmokers at a cocktail party should keep their mouths shut should someone light up. Smokers these days are usually older—in this case that means important—and do not want to be pestered by your petty expression of need for clean air. If you are truly allergic to smoke or are asthmatic, a small cough will alert the smoker to your situation. However, if you are not then asked if the smoke is bothering you, stop there. You will score extra points for tolerance.

Leaving

Just as you weren't the first to arrive, do not be the last to leave. Say good-bye to everyone you spoke to; shake their hands again. The last people you should speak to are, in order, the person who interviewed you, the person who invited you to the party, and the head of the hiring committee. Thank each for inviting you; tell them you had a wonderful time and how nice it was to meet the members of the company. What they say to you at this time will likely indicate how they feel about you.

And that's it. You've done it. Go home and get some rest. You may have to do it again.

Preparing for Questions

To ease your anxiety about interviews, take time to prepare for questions you are likely to encounter and prepare questions you may want to ask. By now, you have spent a considerable amount of time during the career-planning and resume-writing process getting to know yourself, your interests, and your goals. Think about these issues again and about how you will articulate your feelings in the context of an interview. You must be able to express yourself clearly and accurately in positive statements about yourself.

Most interviews begin with some small talk and conversation. The interviewer may ask you, "How is it going?" The best approach is to be friendly and polite, without being overly chummy. An objective of the interview is to get to know you, so be forthcoming and frank without rattling on.

Many students report that interviews with large firms rarely got past this casual conversation mode to more serious questions. Sometimes, interviewers pick things to talk about off the applicant's resume such as traveling, hobbies, or unusual jobs. The interviewer's objective in these cases is not to find out more about bungee jumping, but rather to discover if you can carry on a "normal" conversation. They already know from your resume and transcripts that you are bright and work hard.

Whether the interview is casual or formal, the essential preparation is to read over the resume you sent. Then, keeping in mind one of the companies to which you applied, try to quickly answer the questions below, at least in point form. The goal of this exercise is to simulate the very brief amount of time you will have to answer questions during an interview. When you are done, read over your answers and critique them; make sure the answers highlight your important skills and successfully convey your personality and your career objectives. It is possible that you will be asked none of these questions, but answering them now will prepare you to give verbal answers that incorporate features about yourself that you want to emphasize. It also allows you to eliminate information you wish to remain undisclosed.

Practice Questions

1. Why did you decide to become a "fill-in-the-blank"?

2. Why did you choose ____ school?

3. What were your favorite courses in school? Why?

4. What attracted you to this company?

5. How do you feel your prior work experience will help you in your work here?

6. What are your greatest strengths and weaknesses?

7. What qualities do you feel you possess which will help you in your work as a "fill-in-the-blank"?

8. Do you think your grades are a good indication of your academic achievement? Why or why not?

9. What area of our business interests you most, if any?

10. What are you looking for in an employer?

11. Where do you see yourself several years from now?

12. Is there anything you would like to tell us that was not indicated in the interview or on your resume?

The above questions are rather standard, and you should have your answers ready for all of them. Sometimes, however, your interviewer will ask you questions that seem to throw you a curve. Be prepared. They may be questions like the following:

1. Describe a difficult situation at work and how you handled it. What could you have done differently?

2. Describe your leadership style.

3. Give me an example of your teamwork.

4. What are you most proud of? What are your most important accomplishments?

5. What causes you to worry?

6. Why should we not hire you?

Mature applicants seem to get asked: How would you handle working for people younger than you?

Be aware of what your answers really say to the potential employer. If they ask you where you see yourself in ten years and you have plans to become a trekker, a carpenter, or an investment banker with another firm, do not tell them your plans. Remember that even though the statistics show otherwise, they think they are looking for long-term employees. You haven't even started and they do not want to invest their time and money in you if you're already planning to leave.

Inappropriate Questions

The issue of inappropriate questions being asked in interviews is receiving more attention than ever. A company must walk a fine line. You must be asked enough questions in sufficient detail that the company has adequate information to determine if you would be a good employee. But investigations into your personality and your life cannot cross over into areas that are not pertinent to work. It is irrelevant whether or not you are married, plan to have children, celebrate non-statutory religious holidays, belong to a particular political party, have epilepsy, or wear a turban. Yet, as you may have already guessed, many companies do want to know these things.

It may be a good idea to decide beforehand how you will react if you are made uncomfortable by a line of questioning or a remark. If you feel the interviewer has asked you an inappropriate question, do not be afraid to ask about its relevance to your hiring qualifications. It is also wise to have a prepared response at the ready, one that is inoffensive, friendly, and reasonable.

Government human rights regulations are intended to promote equal opportunity regardless of race, ancestry, place of origin, color, ethnic origin, citizenship, creed, sex, sexual orientation, age, record of criminal offenses, marital status, family status, or handicap. Any questions that deal with these issues must relate to qualifications necessary for the particular job to which you applied. Below is a list of inappropriate questions. Note that some questions may legally be asked after you are offered employment.

Unacceptable Questions

1. Where did you learn to speak German, Arabic, French, etc.?

2. Do you celebrate religious holidays which require time off?

3. How old are you?

4. Have you ever been married? Why? Why not?

5. Do you belong to any political parties?

6. Do you have children or plan to have them?

However, it is acceptable to ask:

1. Do you speak German, Arabic, Mandarin, etc.?

2. Are you legally entitled to work?

3. Would you be available to work on Saturdays and Sundays?

4. Are you between the ages of 18 and 65?

5. Do you wish to be addressed as Mrs., Miss, or Ms.?

6. What do you think of the election coming up?

7. Would you like some information about our maternity leave plan?

As you can see, it could be difficult to distinguish between an unacceptable question and friendly, or at least permissible, conversation. In some cases you may wish to volunteer information. If you are applying at a company with a lot of Pacific Rim exposure, you may want to let them know that not only do you speak Cantonese but that you are also well connected in the Hong Kong business community. Some firms may look favorably upon your Republican association; others may be impressed that you got into banking at the age of sixteen, or seventy.

Women often encounter the majority of unacceptable questions. Because companies are interested in long-term employees and high productivity, they are often inappropriately concerned that a woman's commitment to her work in terms of her time and energy will be lessened by her family plans. They want to know if you are married or intend to have children; as you answer these questions they are calculating the cost to them of your maternity leave or worrying about hiring a replacement.

Apparently, men do not care about their children and never leave their jobs. The guidelines for questions in these areas are unclear; if asked, reveal only what you want. After all, you cannot be expected to predict the future. Most women in the professions suggest that you keep your family plans to yourself during the hiring process. Those plans are your own private business. When asked where you see yourself in ten years, answer in professional terms.

Questions You May Want to Ask

With the availability of company surveys in most any major library, there are several questions which, if asked, indicate that you did or did not do your research. Company surveys include information such as the areas of specialization, salary, weekly hours, and the type of work the company does. Do not ask about these, although you may ask for some elaboration.

It is always a good idea to ask questions; it demonstrates your interest in the company. However, after a certain point, too many questions work against you; you may be seen as arrogant, insincere, pushy, too curious, or too uninformed. And interviewers tend to tell applicants exactly what they want to hear. Get all your important information from another source.

Here are some sample questions for you to consider, along with the stock answers you are likely to hear:

- How would you describe the atmosphere at this company?

   (It is relaxed and friendly, yet businesslike.)

- What are this company's plans for the future?

   (The company is always looking for talented individuals to move up the corporate ladder and to venture into new and exciting areas of business.)

- Is there frequent client contact?

   (We encourage a lot of client contact.)

- Will I have a chance to spend some extra time in the department?

(Oh, yes, we are very flexible.)

- What type of computer system does the company use?

(Gee, I don't know. Let's ask Bob.)

Why bother asking when you know the answer you will get? Well, maybe just to keep the conversation going. Just don't believe everything you're told.

Tips to Get You Through

The most important advice to get you through the interview process is to keep a positive attitude. It may be a stressful, frustrating, and trying time, but you are up to the challenge. Responding to the above sample questions should have made you familiar with the substance of the interview. You should now be prepared for what the company will want to know and how you will answer thoughtfully and articulately. You should also be reasonably confident that you will be able to express yourself and relax (O.K., pretend to relax) during the actual interview. Here are some final hints:

1. Get a good night's rest before an interview; you will need all the energy you can muster.

2. Take along a copy of the resume package you sent, so you can refer to it if the interviewer requires any clarification or offer it if the interviewer needs an extra copy.

3. Never arrive late. In fact, arriving a few minutes early will allow you time to collect your thoughts and to adjust to the setting. You should always leave time to check yourself in a bathroom mirror. Make sure your hair hasn't exploded and that lunch isn't on your clothes or in your teeth. Observe the company at work. Are doors open or closed? How do the executives interact with the support staff? Is it the same way they interact with each other? You can learn a lot by keeping your eyes and ears open.

4. Be respectful and take your cues from the interviewer. Do not enter a room until invited. Be aware of the interviewer's signals that the interview is over. These signals may include repeatedly looking at a watch or clock or asking if you have any final questions.

5. Your resume will serve as the road map for your interview. Know your resume inside-out and be prepared to answer any questions about the experiences you have had. Perfect the story about the typhus you contracted during exam period to explain your low average.

6. Try to establish, in your own mind, what you want to highlight and convey. Remember to SELL BENEFITS to the prospective employer. Take opportunities that arise to do so. It is acceptable to raise something if you would like to discuss it.

7. Smile. Be confident. However, avoid being "chummy," overly gratuitous, or arrogant.

8. Always look the interviewer in the eye as you answer a question. If there are several interviewers, be sure to look around and speak to all of them, making eye contact as you do.

9. Speak clearly and answer all questions to the best of your ability. Don't make the interviewer pull teeth, but try not to ramble. Look to the interviewer for nonverbal cues indicating that you should be finished speaking.

10. Not every interview will be the same. Try to get a sense of the interviewers; work by their rules and mirror their style. If they seem very relaxed and informal, try not to be too formal; a sense of humor about yourself may score points.

11. Be sincere and truthful with your answers. The interviewers have seen many applicants and can see through insincerity. Be yourself. If you're being someone else, and that other person gets the job, you won't be happy doing it.

Critiquing Your Performance

It may help to critique your performance after an interview in order to prepare for the next. Use your Interview Records Forms. You may feel that doing so is being unkind to yourself during this stressfest, but critiquing yourself, or identifying the "Interview Lessons" is good preparation for the next time, and preparation is sure to calm you. Record your meeting immediately after an interview when the experience is still fresh in your mind. Review the Interview Record before your next interview.

The Offer and Your Decision

1. The Less-Than-Perfect Offer

You have done a great deal of work exploring yourself, your values, and your goals and ambitions. And, in the process, you have discovered, there is probably no such thing as the '"perfect" job. Nevertheless, you do want work that is, in some way, on some level, satisfying, or helpful, or gratifying. Perhaps the work will help you with your bills. Maybe it will lead to other contacts and opportunities. It could be that it will add a dimension to your resume that is lacking. Only you can decide if this less-than-perfect offer is one you should accept.

2. Rejections

While rejections are disappointing and often discouraging, they are part of the process and are to be expected. Almost all applicants will be rejected at some stage of the process. It is wise to respond to each rejection with a note thanking the company for considering your application and, if you are still searching for work, a request that your application be kept on file in case of any opportunities that may arise. On the positive side, if you did receive other offers, rejections help narrow the options from which you must choose.

3. Offers

The most common way of making an offer is by telephone. However an offer is made to you (at the end of your interview, by phone, or by mail), be sure to get it in writing at some point.

Acceptance Letter Outline

Date

Name
Title
Company Name
Address

Dear:

Open with a statement naming the job and salary you are accepting.

State the date you plan to begin work and add applicable details if any.

Close with a brief statement of pleasure for the opportunity to work with the company.

Sincerely,

Signature

Typed Full Name

Sample Acceptance Letter

July 15, 1997

John Lassinger
Manager, Product Development
ReRoute Household Products
97 State Street
Atlanta, GA 30319

Dear Mr. Lassinger:

Thank you for offering me a position as a new product manager at ReRoute Household Products at a starting salary of $29,000 annually. I am pleased to accept.

I have given 30 days notice, as required in my current job, and should be settled in Atlanta shortly thereafter. As we agreed, I will report to work on September 1, 1997.

I look forward to a long and successful career at ReRoute.

Sincerely,

Fred Foster

Fred Foster

Evaluating the Company

The company has spent a good deal of time evaluating you; you owe it to yourself to also evaluate them.

Ask yourself:

- Did the interviewer ask relevant and interesting questions?

- Did people listen thoughtfully to my answers?

- Did the interviewer give a sales pitch? Was it convincing?

- Was I encouraged to contact the interviewer or another person if I had any further questions?

- Was I shown around the premises?

- How were people interacting?

- Was the interview a pleasant experience?

- Were the people I met people with whom I would like to work?

- Would I be proud to be associated with this company?

- Would I feel comfortable having these people as partners?

- What are the prospects for advancement?

- Is the salary fair?

- Is the working environment one in which I feel comfortable or to which I could adapt?

- Do I like this place and these people?

- Does this place fit with my values?

- Are the benefits adequate?

Making Tough Decisions

Beware of a pack mentality; don't join up just because everyone else thinks it's a good idea. Business and industry are not immune to fads, and every year there are one or two that, for whatever reason, become very trendy. You are the one who has to work so be sure that your decision is based on reasons that make sense to you.

Also, be wary of hard sells. Just as you are marketing yourself, the company is marketing itself to you, and it has far more experience than you do. Talk to friends. One company may have had a really terrific interviewer who charmed every applicant who walked through the door by giving each the same lines. Weigh all the factors: benefits vs. atmosphere; personal attention vs. hands-on experience. Unfortunately, you can never know everything and will have to rely on your instincts.

Try to make a decision with which you will be comfortable for a year. If you do accept an offer, do so in person or by telephone and always follow up in writing. If you have received numerous offers, be sure to contact all of them, thanking them for their consideration and offer. It is not necessary to tell a company you have declined which offer you have accepted.

If initially you are unable to secure precisely the work you want, keep a positive attitude, an eye to the want ads, and a flourishing network. Contact your resources so you are in a good position to follow up on job vacancies as soon as they become known.

Conclusion

Once again, by knowing the information, by knowing yourself, and by being yourself, you will find satisfying work. This may be a difficult or an exciting time depending on how you look at it. So keep your wits about you and stay positive.

Tips for Effective Interviewing

I'm not afraid of death. It's just that I don't want to be there when it happens.

—Woody Allen

Olsten Staffing Services of Melville, New York (on the Web at www.olsten.com) offers the following tips which provide a good summary and are reprinted here with permission.

TIPS FOR EFFECTIVE INTERVIEWING ©1996 OLSTEN CORPORATION

1. Knowledge of a potential employer's business will never fail to impress! Research the company beforehand. Get a recent annual report and become familiar with the contents. Read newspaper or magazine articles on the company and its industry. If possible, speak to people in other companies in the same industry.

2. Rehearse for the interview and be prepared to do about 75% of the talking. An interviewer will want to see how effectively you can express yourself and how knowledgeable you are about the industry.

3. Cite specific examples of how your past professional experience relates to the position for which you are applying and how your skills relate to the company's needs.

4. Ask questions about the company and the position to demonstrate your interest and initiative.

5. Don't ask about benefits on the first interview; instead, concentrate on stressing how you can make a contribution to your prospective employer's organization.

Leaping Tall Buildings and Other Barriers

It isn't changes that do you in, it's the transitions.
—William Bridges

Of course, there may be barriers out there, but you have labored to deepen your awareness of yourself and to expand your appreciation of the options available to you. So, whatever you choose, you know you've got the tools to do it!

After all this work, should you still feel you want to work for someone else, the following rules apply:

1. **Prepare. Prepare. Prepare.**

From your initial analysis of your personal style, skills, and values to the crafting of your resume and through your contact list, preparation is key.

2. **Be true to yourself.**

That's what career planning is all about.

3. **Sell benefits.**

In your interviews, establish rapport and SELL BENEFITS. It's not enough to list your skills on a resume or to say what you have accomplished. Turn these attributes into benefits for the prospective employer.

4. **Keep records.**

These will prove invaluable for later reference.

5. **Follow up.**

- Make notes of leads and follow them through.

- Remember your thank you notes.

- Call after an interview if you haven't heard back in a reasonable amount of time.

6. **Get feedback.**

If you do not get the job, don't be discouraged. Use it as a learning opportunity; call the interviewer for feedback. Interviewers are usually extremely responsive to these calls, and the information you receive may be just what you need to be successful next time.

Endnotes

1. Contributed by Bram Lebo, LLB, MBA, MBI.

JOB SEARCH TECHNIQUES:
TRIED AND TRUE, OLD AND NEW

As you search for work, keep in mind that in America today, 39 million people are working from home, 20 million of them running their own home-based business. And by the time this book goes to print, those numbers will have increased substantially. The moral—the work you want may be as close as your home computer.

Network: Access Your Allies

The fact is, you are already connected to the labor market. Throughout the last weeks or months, on the job or in your job search, while talking with others or while working through this book, you have also been chatting with people, meeting people, reading about people, and hearing about them, too. These people are your network. It is often through your network that you will find work.

There are a number of ways to help you get a handle on what your network looks like and who can be counted in it. Some people like to make lists. Others prefer creating file cards and devising a system for cross referencing. One method we like is "mapping."

Map Your Network

1. Begin with the name of someone you know well and place it in the center of a page, flip chart, or blackboard. Circle it. Write the person's job/connections below.

2. From that initial circle, make branches of other names that come to mind and of their work/connections.

3. Keep going until your page or board is filled with names and work/connections.

4. Stick your map someplace where you will see it often, and add to it over a period of several days.

5. When you think you've remembered everyone in your network, begin to look for work/connections that "fit" with what you want and start making calls. You may find that some people pass you on to others, but that's fine; you've got another name to add to your network. Start talking, questioning, and setting up meetings.

Expand Your Network

To expand and explore your network:

1. Find out who belongs to what organization and why; you may discover it is useful to join, too.

2. Ask what industry magazines or journals people read regularly; you may discover they are a rich source of potential job information.

3. Learn what conferences, seminars, or public meetings people attend and why; you might find these semi-structured occasions ideal opportunities to network.

List Your Network

If you are still having difficulty recognizing your network possibilities, the following list may help.

1. Friends and family

   - who work in an organization or industry of interest to you

   - who know people who work in an organization or industry of interest to you

   - who are well-connected former employees or business associates.

2. People with contacts

   - doctors
   - lawyers
   - stock brokers
   - teachers
   - clergy
   - insurance agents
   - head hunters
   - dentists
   - bankers
   - politicians
   - accountants
   - civic leaders
   - temporary help agencies

3. Organizations

   - church/synagogue groups
   - brotherhoods/sisterhoods
   - political parties

- Elks, Rotary Clubs, Masons, etc.

- PTA

- hobby associations

4. Professional or industrial organizations

   - professional societies

   - alumni groups

   - unions or trade groups

   - chambers of commerce

5. Publications

   - newspaper ads

   - newspaper articles

   - professional or industrial journals

   - company newsletters

   - career libraries

   - periodicals (e.g., *Forbes*)

   - annual reports

   - placement offices

   - recruiting brochures

   - case studies

   - trade publications

   - directories

- Department of Labor *Occupational Outlook Handbook*

- Internet bulletin boards and job lists

In terms of networking, once again, Wendy Enelow (http://amsquare.com/america/advantag/winning.html) has written a super on-line article, *Using Your Contacts to Find Job Leads*, which just might provide the motivation you need. Her article is excerpted here with permission.

Using Your Contacts

Ever talk to your boss from 10 years ago? Your co-workers from your last job? The neighbor you met last summer at the block party? The new coach at the tennis club? Your banker? Your hair dresser? The list goes on and on.

These individuals and many more are your single best source of employment contact in today's job market. Long gone are the days when you were able to pick up the newspaper, select ten good advertisements, mail resumes, and get five offers. Today, in order to job search effectively, you need to be aggressive, visible, and determined.

Often individuals out of work, for whatever reason, are "embarrassed" to let others know that they are in the job market. It's not their fault...times are difficult. However, we have all been brought up in a society where our self-esteem is directly related to our professional lives. We lose our jobs, and we feel inadequate, no matter the reason.

It's often difficult to put these feelings aside, realize that downsizings and other negative activity in the job market is directly affecting thousands and thousands of individuals, and appreciate the critical impact and success of networking to identify job opportunities. The opportunities are there, the only problem is that they are no longer listed in the newspaper or through professional recruiters. It's time to speak up.

Developing your network of contacts is no mystery. It's hard work and constant communication. Each and every person you come in contact with, from the gentleman you meet in line at the post office to the manager of your favorite restaurant, can be an excellent source of employment contact. It's often amazing what other people know about job opportunities. And the only way that you are going to find out about this information is to speak up and let EVERYONE know that you are in the job market. Believe me, they won't think it's your fault. They'll be sympathetic and often remarkably helpful.

Have you thought about the fact that...

Commercial real estate agents are aware of new companies moving into the area, companies moving into larger facilities, and new leases that have been signed? Bankers are also aware of new companies in the area, new contracts that have been awarded, new products that are ready to hit the market and so much more? Restaurant managers know all about their regular customers—their jobs, their successes at work, their travel to develop new clients, new sales they have won, and the "scuttlebutt" about company acquisitions and mergers.

Professional association meetings and conferences are one of the single most effective methods to job search. Join your industry's professional associations, and you'll walk into a room filled with individuals, all of whom are potential contacts for job search leads. This can be an extremely effective method to rapidly expand your network of contacts.

Civic associations and community groups are also an excellent source of networking contacts. Again, a room full of individuals, all potential sources of job information, are at your immediate disposal. How much easier can it be?

Equally important is your ability to network yourself into a company. If you know that you are interested in working for the ABC Company, call the company and establish communication with an individual at the firm—the human resource director, the sales and marketing manager, the purchasing director, or the receptionist. Anyone will do. In fact, I recommend that at this initial stage you bypass the human resources department. These individuals are often overwhelmed with potential candidates, and you just become one of the maddening crowd.

But how many times has someone really worked to establish a relationship with the receptionist, the warehouse manager, or the engineer? Call these individuals, tell them that you have heard about the ABC Company and that you wanted to find out some information about the firm directly from an individual who is employed there. Ask about their job, their responsibilities, and their successes. People love to talk about themselves and share their ideas. Once you've established the contact, now you have an entry in the door.

Informational interviews can also be a great source of networking. Call a company and tell them you are exploring opportunities with numerous firms in the area and would like to get some information about their company. Don't ask for a job interview, just ask for information—information about job opportunities with the company and information about opportunities with other companies that they may be aware of. You will be amazed at the results.

Most important, use your job interviews to develop leads. Hopefully, each interview will reap an offer.

However, let's be realistic. In today's job market that is often not the case. I recommend that when you leave each interview, you take with you the names of three to five companies (or individuals) to add to your network. When your interview is winding down, tell the interviewer that you are quite interested in employment with his or her company (if that is the case), but do they know of anyone else who may be interested in a candidate with your qualifications.

To support your networking campaign, develop a network contact lead tracking system (I recommend 3 × 5 index cards). Each and every time you get a lead, complete a card with full name, company, address, telephone, and fax. Mail your resume, mark the mailing date on the card, and place it into a tickler file for follow up in one week. And make that follow-up call. It is a proven fact that:

Individuals who follow up once they have mailed a resume will be more successful in their job search campaign. Networking is the key to success. Set goals for yourself—five new contacts per week, ten new contacts, whatever is most realistic for you. If you establish only three new contacts each week and get three more from each of those individuals, before long you will have a wealth of networking and contact information leading you successfully to your next position.

Scour the Newspapers

Traditionally, the want ads in your local newspaper were a rich source of job postings for the hunter. In addition, many cities print weekly or monthly publications dedicated to job listings. But because of the sheer numbers of people looking for work, these resources are less useful than they once were. Indeed, when you apply to one or another of the posted ads, you may find yourself among hundreds of others who were similarly moved. Still, it's worth checking through the ads on a regular basis—you never know who might be looking for you!

Target Head Hunters

These are the agencies that recruit on behalf of the companies they represent. Should an agency make a successful match between a company and a new hire, it is the hiring company that pays for the service, not you.

Most often, head hunting agencies are searching for highly paid professionals they can place in a senior position for a hefty fee, but not always. With the tightened economy and trimmed internal resources in many industries—so that companies have neither the time nor the personnel to do their own recruiting—the head hunting business is thriving. It could be well worth your while to send your resume to two or three of these agencies, and while you are looking, they, too, can search for work you can do.

Should you decide to work with head hunters, you may want to ask some questions such as:

1. Whom do you represent?

2. How many people did you successfully place last year?

3. Who pays your fee?

4. At what levels do you usually place people?

5. How much do you know about my industry/area?

6. What can I expect from your agency?

7. Do you have a data base?

8. How do you network? With other recruiters?

Try Temporary Help Agencies

Temporary help agencies are busier than ever filling slots in a broad variety of businesses. Registering with one or more of these agencies may keep you working for a long time, albeit in consecutive positions. Check your local Yellow Pages for a list of temporary help agencies and look in the want ads to learn which agencies are most active in your community or city.

Richard's experience with a temp agency paid off in an unusual but positive way. A skilled human resources professional in a major bank, Richard had enjoyed working in the same position for eleven years when he unexpectedly found himself the casualty of a huge corporate reorganization. Suddenly, he was told his job was redundant. And, while he was given a severance package of six months pay, at 55, Richard was out of work and frightened.

Richard began networking and making as many contacts as he could, but it appeared to him that there was little "out there" in his field. True, he was offered a number of positions, but on a variety of levels, none of them appeared to fit.

Fearful he would never find work, his severance and savings exhausted, Richard pulled out the Yellow Pages and started to search through the temporary agencies listed there. In speaking with one agency, he quickly learned that they restricted themselves to placing only secretarial and administrative staff; Richard saw a niche for himself.

Richard went directly to the president of the agency and presented a well-conceived proposal for broadening the company's market. Knowing what he knew about big companies, both from his previous work and from his year of job-search contacts, and recognizing that, commonly, in any newly pruned and reorganized company there is an urgent need for short-term expertise, Richard was in a position to make a real contribution to the agency. In addition, Richard believed he had the transferable skills to make him an ideal professional recruiter. The president agreed, and Richard got the job.

Should you decide to work with temporary agencies, you may want to ask some questions such as:

1. Whom do you represent?

2. How much work did the average person get from your agency last year?

3. Who pays your fee?

4. At what levels do you usually place people?

5. How much do you know about my industry/area?

6. What can I expect from your agency?

7. Do you have a data base?

8. How do you network?

Nontraditional Job Search Techniques—A Better Mousetrap

If you have always done it that way, it's probably wrong.
—Charles Kettering

If you've been looking for work in all the usual places, chances are you have not been successful in reaching your goal. The business buzz is that you will have to be creative in your search for work or at least set out on a few of the less well-worn paths.

1. Network through the Internet

Only two years ago, this method of networking did not even exist, or if it did, it was relegated to the super-techno-pros. Today, a simple PC and a modem put you in the business of cyber-networking. Yes, you can use the World Wide Web as a resource. Not only can you find job postings of every kind and description, you can post your own resume in cyberspace. Indeed, you can give, gather, or get information of any description.

Be creative about how you use the Web, and you may be delightfully surprised at the results. For example, Jan, a writer we know, had a long list of credits in the nonfiction and technical writing field. But, given the tightened economy, Jan was having difficulty finding sufficient work in her usual arena. She decided to try her hand at screen writing, only to discover that it is next to impossible to get a *property* read without an agent.

Jan decided to try the Net and started her exploration in the usual way. Using a search engine to scour the Net, she punched in the Key Words "screenwriting agent." To her dismay, Jan found hundreds of agents who handled everything from import/export to houses for sale but not a single agent who dealt with scripts. She tried again, this time punching in the words "film agent." The results were not much better for the word "agent," but "film" turned up some interesting leads.

Following these new leads, Jan now discovered a "Hollywood connection." There, she found dozens of bulletin boards, many of which used a question and answer format. And most of these bulletin boards, or networks, were moderated by an honest-to-goodness certified pro—Hollywood producers, script doctors, and directors—the kind of people Jan had hoped to engage but never expected to meet. And now, she was able to e-mail them personally and directly with her question: how do I find an agent?

The pros responded, and in a matter of days, Jan had three reasonable and specific avenues to pursue, three concrete solutions she would never have imagined on her own.

So, use the Web as an effective aid to your own job search and do some on-line research. Find job postings, access the pros, and discover key information about the industry or company that interests you. Advertise yourself by creating a Web site of your own and linking yourself to the search engines and to others who may be looking for precisely your talents and expertise. Send out trial balloons in the form of questions, and your new cyberpals will not let you down; they will respond. Enlarge your network and your opportunities through the Net!

2. Advertise

Placing an ad in the newspaper is not what we mean here, although that does work occasionally. We're talking creative approaches to making yourself, your talents, or your services known. This could include anything from printing up fliers and dropping them in the appropriate mail slots, to setting up an interesting stand at the corner of Main Street, to taking a booth and promoting yourself or your services at a local flea market, to filming your own video and distributing it to potential clients.

3. Try temporary help agencies

You may already know that in the United States, Manpower is bigger than General Motors in terms of the number of employees and profits. Manpower is simply another temporary help agency; there are many others, and, traditionally, they've been used by people looking for temporary work.

But there is a new twist to the old story. Employers are more fearful than ever of hiring someone who cannot do the job. Many employers do not trust the sparkling resumes they read; they want proof a worker has the competencies and the personality to fit in. So, they hire on a temporary basis with the long-term view of keeping the temp employee permanently, if they work out. In other words, employers have begun to use temporary help agencies to screen for good candidates.

Consider a temporary help agency for three good reasons:

1. a temporary job may lead to permanent work;

2. it's a good way to get yourself known;

3. it helps pay the bills.

TAKE A NEW ROUTE: WORK FOR YOURSELF

If a man knows not what harbor he seeks,
any wind is the right wind.

---

1. Become a "portfolio worker"

You may want to generate several sources of income potential at the same time. Develop flexibility. There is no reason you can't have half a dozen business cards in your pocket, each selling you or your services in very different and distinct markets. Sell gardening services, leather goods, how-to carpentry books, recipes, and cleaning services, all at the same time. Explore the marketplace and learn to track trends; sell people what they want. Become a "multipreneur."

2. Become an entrepreneur

Market yourself for today's reality. For an ever growing number of people, job hopping has become a way of life and continuous change is the only real constant. Self-employment, contract work, portfolio work, and home-based businesses provide endless opportunities for income.

3. Start a home-based business

Dorothea Helms, a principal of Write Stuff Writing Services (http://www.enterprise.ca/~helms/), began a successful writing career at the age of 40. Wise to the ways of at-home business, Helms says, "Don't let working out of your home be a competitive disadvantage." In addition, she warns, "You can do it all...but, who wants to?" The following advice is reprinted with Helms' permission.

Minding Your Business...At Home

1. Get help for those things you don't like to do.

    • Cleaning help isn't as expensive as you think.

    • Pay someone to help with your business.

    • Time management is critical.

    • Your time is as valuable as anyone else's in business.

    • Take time to exercise, sleep, and eat well.

    • Keep a central calendar and keep it up-to-date.

    • Try to organize as much as possible and save time.

    • Let the answering machine do its job.

2. If you want to get paid as a professional...act like one.

    • Prepare an office or workspace that is yours.

    • Answer the phone in a professional manner.

    • If you deal with the public a lot by phone or in person, consider day care for small children during your peak business hours.

    • Invest in some business clothing appropriate to your work.

    • Keep your equipment current and in good repair.

3. Keep your business life in perspective.

- Try to separate your business and personal lives.

- Try to keep your children's lives as consistent as possible. Make time for yourself and your spouse/life partner.

- Ask for family members' help with the business if appropriate.

- Neither the world nor your business will end if you take a vacation.

- Not everyone in business will necessarily like you.

4. Charge enough for your product or service to make money.

- Remember that some jobs pay in ways other than money.

- Don't be afraid to turn down work that's not worth it.

- So you're home-based? You've still got overhead! Don't give work away.

5. Some general tips:

- Get business cards printed and USE THEM!

- Avoid vertical formats; stick to a plainer format.

- GET OUT THERE AND NETWORK! Consider:

  Internet

  Newspaper-based on-line services

  Courses

  Seminars, workshops

  Home shows (whether working or attending)

Clubs

Volunteer organizations

Support groups

Trade journals

Media

Trade shows

Word-of-mouth: talk, talk, talk; listen, listen, listen.

4. Create a "virtual company"

Research your market and link yourself with others whose expertise is different from but collateral to yours. For example, if you are good at gardening, align yourself with some nurseries, fence or deck builders, and pool construction companies. If you have a flair for decorating, you may want to affiliate with fabric shops, tile manufacturers, carpet salespeople and carpenters. If you want to arrange parties, hook up with church or synagogue groups, printers, and disc jockeys.

In the 21st century, career success will be won by people who understand and practice old-fashioned customer service—giving people what they want.

Motivational Tips

When you feel overwhelmed by the job search process—and who doesn't from time to time—all you may need is a few reminders to help keep your spirits up. Nancy Alrichs of E-Span, a company committed to serving individual job seekers and human resource professionals (http://www.espan.com/docs/telefon.html), reminds you that, "A job search requires ongoing replenishment of your 'motivation reserves'. These are a natural part of a job search. Staying motivated day to day is a trick that can be learned!" Alrichs also suggests you read these motivators and "add your own to the end of the list for energizing ideas." Excerpts from Alrichs' on-line article are reprinted here with permission.

Rule Number One: Don't sweat the small stuff.

Rule Number Two: It's all small stuff.

Every "no" gets you closer to "yes."

Just do it!

This is the Crisis du Jour. By this time next week, you won't even remember it.

By putting faith into action, those doubts, fears, and worries can be overcome and goals achieved.

Change means CHANGE. If you always do what you've always done, you'll always get what you've always gotten in the past.

Motivation: 15 Ways to Feel Great Every Day

1. Feel good about who you are. Trying to be someone else or someone you or others believe you should be wastes energy. Accept yourself.

2. Use positive self-talk. Make good things happen by saying, "I want to," "I have decided to," "I deserve to," instead of "I should." Think thoughts that move you closer to your goals instead of putting up roadblocks.

3. Associate with positive people. Attitudes are contagious. Surround yourself with energy givers, not energy drainers.

4. Set a positive pace for the day. Start the day with music. Play an upbeat song, tune in to a radio station with energizing music or sing out loud to get your adrenaline pumping.

5. Take vitamins. A single multivitamin provides a subtle boost to your energy.

6. Exercise regularly. If you don't already exercise regularly, start walking 20 minutes a day. Watch your energy soar!

7. Accept your cycles. During low energy periods, pursue job hunting activities that require less effort. Prioritize tasks to take advantage of your peak energy times.

8. Eat a balanced diet.

9. Don't obsess over your (seeming lack of) progress. Rather than tell yourself that "I MUST get this particular job," tell yourself, "I would like this job, but if I don't get it, I will pursue a similar position with their competition." Or say, "While I am waiting for so-and-so to call me back, I can research a few more logical contacts."

10. Avoid perfectionism. Progress, don't try to perfect.

11. Get enough sleep. Sleep recharges you! Staying up late means sleeping in late and late sleepers miss connecting with the people who can help.

12. Chart your progress in steps. Getting a job is not the only measure of forward progress. A phone call to set up a meeting is progress. A networking meeting is progress. An interview or offer—even one you decline—is progress.

13. Reward yourself. Plan two fun "events" per week.

14. Join a professional group. Professional groups exist to sharpen their members' skills and to assist with their career transitions. To find the right group for you, go to the library and consult the Directory of Professional Associations. While you are there, check the Sunday and Monday issues of your local newspaper or business journal. Read the list of meetings in your area. Even an old issue has good information about who to call for reservations. Call and ask to be a guest of the person taking the reservations (but offer to pay your own way). You will be introduced to other members and learn more about the group quickly. Your next employer could be in that group!

15. Seek out a group of job seekers like yourself. Everyone in the group will have a rolodex and a brain. Job seekers help each other with the exchange of job leads, insights about particular companies, and emotional support.

Final Messages

Instead of deciding what you want to be when you grow up, you must ask and re-ask yourself what kinds of things you want to do now and later.

Remember that:

- change is constant

- continuous learning will serve you well

- knowing your heart promotes life satisfaction

- life and goals change

- allies help

- flexibility helps

- it is the journey, not the destination, that fills your life.

And **THINC DEEP**

Take control of the decision-making process.

Hold on to your values.

Identify your needs and wants.

Navigate through all the information and look at alternatives, advantages, and disadvantages.

Calculate the risk.

Determine your likelihood of satisfaction.

Evaluate the work and its ramifications.

Eliminate any option you can't live with regardless of its short-term attractiveness.

Prepare, prepare, prepare, and pick your spot.

24

CAREER ACTION PLAN

You've done it! You have read the book, focused in, looked out, visioned, explored, clarified, networked, and outreached. You have completed the process of single tracking your vision with your reality, and you have written reams and reams of notes. It's time to write your Career Action Plan.

A concrete **Career Action Plan** ensures that:

1. You have a step-by-step plan for attacking your career development design.

2. You have an easy-to-use vehicle for tracking quantitative and qualitative results.

3. You tie your personal profile to your career goals.

4. You make a solid commitment to career planning and personal growth.

Your Action Plan should detail at least five Key Goals and identify the specific action steps you will take, the measurements you will use to track your progress, the date you hope to complete the steps, and the strategies you will use in pursuit of your Key Goals. Use the following Career Action Plan outline to record your plan; update and revise as required.

Career Action Plan Implementation

1. When your Action Plan is completed, it is a good idea to meet with a friend or mentor, someone you can count on to be supportive, someone you trust to give you honest and helpful feedback in discussing your plans.

2. Include traditional and nontraditional approaches in your job search Action Plan.

3. When you take your Action Plan to your supporter for discussion, be sure your resume or Marketing Package highlights the "added value" you as a unique individual will bring to a job; it is important that your supporter understand your strategies for proper feedback to occur.

GOOD LUCK!

This is it.
The end is the journey.

Career Action Plan

Key Goal #1

Action Step(s):

Measurements:

Completion Date:

Strategies:

Key Goal #2

Action Step(s):

Measurements:

Completion Date:

Strategies:

Key Goal #3

Action Step(s):

Measurements:

Completion Date:

Strategies:

Key Goal #4

Action Step(s):

Measurements:

Completion Date:

Strategies:

Key Goal #5

Action Step(s):

Measurements:

Completion Date:

Strategies:

Suggested Reading

Beating Job Burnout: How to Turn Your Work into Your Passion by Paul Stevens (1995, VGM Career Horizons).

Career Crafting by Howard Sambol (ENCOMPASS).

Stop Postponing the Rest of Your Life by Paul Stevens (Ten Speed Press).

The On-Line Job Search Companion by James C. Gonyea (McGraw-Hill).

TOP SECRET Resumes & Cover Letters by Steven Provenzano (1995, Dearborn Publishing).

INDEX